Vive le Tour!

Vive le Tour!

Amazing tales of the Tour de France

Nick Brownlee

PORTICO

First published in the United Kingdom in 2007 by
Portico Books
10 Southcombe Street
London
W14 0RA

An imprint of Anova Books Company Ltd

This edition published in 2010.

ISBN: 1 86105 998 1

ISBN 13: 978 1861059987

A CIP catalogue record for this book is available from the British Library.

10 9 8 7 6 5 4 3 2 1

Typeset by SX Composing DTP, Rayleigh, Essex.
Reproduction by Spectrum Colour Limited, Ipswich.
Printed by Bell & Bain Ltd, Glasgow

This book can be ordered direct from the publisher.
Contact the marketing department, but try your bookshop first.

www.anovabooks.com

CONTENTS

FOREWORD

When I first started writing this book in 2007 it was to coincide with the time trial Prologue and Grand Départ of the Tour de France from London.

As I began jotting down my first notes, I could only hope that interest in the race would be greater than in 1974, when Britain last hosted the Grand Départ. On that day just a few thousand die-hards bothered to watch the likes of Eddy Merckx and Raymond Poulidor racing up and down the Plympton bypass in the rain.

As it turned out few, especially me, could have anticipated how a country traditionally so indifferent to the world's greatest sporting event would be so irrevocably gripped by Tour fever.

Before the race, the incumbent Mayor of London, Ken Livingstone, claimed the event would be a timely riposte to the terrorists who, exactly two years earlier, had detonated bombs on the Underground.

But to those watching by the roadside or on TV, it was clear that this was more than simply a display of Blitz spirit by plucky Londoners. This was an entire country embracing a unique sporting occasion.

Even now it is impossible to calculate just how many people thronged the streets of the capital and the road to Canterbury during those two crazy July days. Was it four million? Was it five?

'These scenes will remain with me forever,' said a clearly stunned Tour organiser Christian Prudhomme as the peloton headed back across the Channel — and he wasn't the only hardened continental to be blown away by the sheer force of British enthusiasm.

What had changed in the 23 years since Plympton, I wondered?

Vive le Tour!

Where had all these people come from?

My thought at the time was that the London Départ was symbolic of a fresh start for the Tour after the debacle of the previous year, when Floyd Landis was stripped of his yellow jersey in Paris.

Things could only get better, I thought, because the sport was on its knees. The dopers had been scourged, there was renewed optimism in the air, and there was even a chance of a British stage winner after decades of non-achievement.

Three years later, I now understand that London was merely the beginning of a period of sustained bloodletting unprecedented in the 107 years of the event; one which, thankfully, has left the Tour in the best shape it has ever been in.

Cheating is not a new phenomenon. In this book, as well as stories of mind-boggling endurance, courage and sporting brilliance, you will find instances of ingenious skulduggery going back to the very earliest days of the Tour.

From Hippolyte Acouturier attaching himself to the back of a support car by his teeth in 1904 to Michel Pollentier using a bladder full of someone else's urine to fool the doping control in 1978, it's almost part of the charm.

But for many the 2006 race – in which Landis's astonishing solo breakaway into Morzine was proved to have been illegally fuelled by testosterone ('Say it ain't so, Floyd.') – represented a new low.

And indeed it was. But it was also the moment when a line was finally drawn in the sand.

By humiliating the hallowed yellow jersey on the Champs Elysee the Tour had sent a definitive message that no-one was safe anymore. The cosy dope club was being dismantled from the top down.

In 2007, relentless in-race testing saw favourites Alexandre

Vinokourov and Michael Rasmussen booted out, the Astana team withdrawn, and a cloud of suspicion hanging over the integrity of the eventual winner, Alberto Contador, even if nothing was proven.

The cull would continue in 2008 — and suddenly teams began to wise up to the fact that the Tour meant business. More importantly, sponsors let it be known that they no longer wished to be associated with teams that cheated.

The result? 2009's race was the cleanest in history, in which a new generation of young riders was able to compete on equal terms for the first time. Suddenly the sport had new heroes — and in Bradley Wiggins and Mark Cavendish, two of them were British. Even the return of Lance Armstrong, like Banquo's ghost, could not faze the tyros. It made for compelling viewing.

So as I look forward to races in the near future, and for years to come, I always remember back to those crowds in the Mall and the roads of Kent in 2007 and believe that was the moment when the Tour de France, despite all the scandals and controversy of the past, truly became something the whole world would embrace for generations to follow.

Vive le Tour!

Nick Brownlee

'Today, my brothers, we gather here in common celebration of the divine bicycle. Not only do we owe it our most pious gratitude for the precious and ineffable love that it has given us, but also for the host of memories sown over our whole sports life and which today has made concrete. In my own case I love it for its having given me a soul capable of appreciating it; I love it for having taken my heart within its spokes, for having encircled a part of my life within its harmonious frame, and for having constantly illuminated me with the victorious sparkle of its nickel plates. In the history of humanity, does it not constitute the first successful effort of intelligent life to triumph over the laws of weights?'

Henri Desgrange, the father of the Tour de France

A BRIEF GLOSSARY OF CYCLING TERMS

Abandon: When a rider quits during a race, usually due to injury. Sprint specialists will often abandon the Tour once it hits the mountains.

Attack: A sudden acceleration to move ahead of another rider or group of riders. These most commonly occur on mountain ascents.

Autobus: A group of non-climbers, usually sprinters, who help each other through the arduous mountain stages by riding together at the back of the peloton.

Bidon: Water bottle.

Bonk: Total exhaustion caused by lack of sufficient food during a long race or ride. Also known as the 'Hunger Knock'. At its most extreme, it can cause light-headedness and even hallucinations.

Break/Breakaway: A rider or group of riders that has left the main group behind.

Classics Race: A one-day race, usually staged in spring. Examples include: Milan–San Remo, Bastogne–Liège–Bastogne, Paris–Roubaix.

Commissaire: A race marshal, who usually follows the riders in a car.

Domestique: A team rider who will sacrifice his individual performance to help the team leader by chasing down breaks and shielding the boss from the wind. Also known as 'water carrier', due to his main duty of keeping the team supplied with water bottles from the team car.

Drop/Dropped: When a rider has been passed by another, or left behind. 'Cracked' is when a rider dramatically runs out of steam, usually on a tough mountain stage.

Bunch Sprint: A mass sprint at the finish of a flat stage, often at speeds in excess of 37.2 mph (60 kph).

Gap: The amount of time or distance between a rider or group of riders and another rider or group of riders.

General Classification (GC/GC): The overall leader board for the race, representing each rider's total cumulative time in the race.

Giro d'Italia: The three-week Tour of Italy which takes place in May and early June. Riders who have achieved the Giro–Tour de France double include Fausto Coppi of Italy and Belgium's Eddie Merckx.

Grand Départ: The moment when the peloton sets off on the Tour.

Gruppetto: A group of riders that forms at the back of the field on mountain stages, riding at a pace that allows them to finish just inside the time limit. Usually, the gruppetto is comprised of sprinters and other riders who are not climbing specialists or race leaders. *Gruppetto* is Italian for 'small group'.

Grande Boucle: The 'Big Loop', another name for the Tour de France.

KoM: King of the Mountains. Awarded to the best climber.

Lanterne Rouge: 'Red Lamp' the last rider to finish a stage.

Maillot Jaune: The 'Yellow Jersey' worn by the race leader in the Tour de France.

Peloton: The main field, or pack, of riders in the race. *Peloton* is French for a 'group moving forward'.

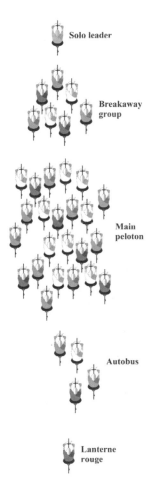

Solo leader

Breakaway group

Main peloton

Autobus

Lanterne rouge

Vive le Tour

Soigneur: General team factotum, responsible for everything from massages to carrying the luggage to and from hotel rooms. The most famous *soigneur* was Willy Voet, who was found to be carrying boxes of doping products in the back of his car (see The Festina Affair, page 210.)

Team: The Tour is made up of twenty professional, sponsored teams drawn from the year-long ProTour circuit, plus any wildcard teams chosen at the discretion of the Tour organisers. Each team consists of nine riders.

Team Leader: The top rider in a team, or at least the one believed to stand the best chance of winning.

Time Trial: A race in which riders start individually and race against the clock. The fastest over a set distance is the winner. Also known as a 'Race of Truth'.

UCI: *Union Cycliste Internationale*, the international governing body of cycling.

Vuelta: The three week Tour of Spain, usually run in September.

THE JERSEYS OF THE TOUR DE FRANCE

Yellow jersey for the General Time Classification (best overall time).

Polka-dot jersey for the Best Climber Classification (points earned at the tops of climbs) – the King of the Mountains.

Green jersey for the General Points Classification (points earned for sprints).

White jersey for the Best Young Rider, awarded to the best rider aged 25 and under.

SCANDALS AND ASSASSINS 1903–1914

'When I feel bad I attack – that way no one can find out how bad I feel.'

Bernard Hinault, five-times Tour winner

'In this business you cannot afford sentiment or else you'll be flattened.'

Marcel Bidot, 1920s French professional and later team manager

'The ideal Tour would be a Tour in which only one rider survived the ordeal.'

Henri Desgrange

THE PROLOGUE

The Prologue is a short race against the clock, usually no more than 6 miles (10 km), in which Tour fans get their first opportunity to see their heroes in action as they set off at two-minute intervals on their time-trial bikes. Although the result of the Prologue counts towards the final classification, it is generally regarded as a means of heralding the start of the Tour, and often takes place in countries outside France. In 2007, the Prologue takes place in London for the first time.

THE LONG ROAD

Long distance road races – the precursor to the Tour – were hugely popular in France in the late nineteenth century. And they really were long distance. In 1891, Charles Terront completed the 736 mile (1,185 km) Paris–Brest–Paris race in just 71 hours – a remarkable achievement considering the state of the roads and the fact he was riding a cumbersome steel bike weighing 9.5 lb (21 kg), fitted with new-fangled pneumatic tyres which punctured five times. An indication of the rapid improvement in bike manufacture came ten years later, when Maurice Garin rode the same course in a comparatively lightning-quick 52 hours.

JOYEUX'S LOOPY ACHIEVEMENT

In 1895 Terront, arguably cycling's first superstar, announced a bold plan to ride all the way around France – on a motorcycle. However, his thunder was stolen in May of that year by one Théophile Joyeux, who set off to complete *le Grande Boucle* (the Big Loop) on his bicycle. Nineteen days later, Joyeux completed his epic journey. He had covered 2,800 miles (4,500 km) at an average of 146 miles (235 km) a day.

TOUR TRIVIA

James Moore of Bury St Edmunds won the first recognised bike race, in Paris in 1868.

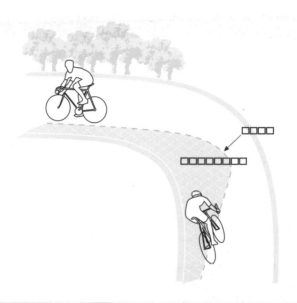

HAIRPINS

One of the great skills of the top Tour rider is being able to descend
hairpin mountain bends in excess of 80 kph (60 mph), using only
minimal braking. The technique, illustrated here, relies upon the rider
moving out towards the far side of the road, braking slightly, then
sweeping round in a parabola in order to keep the 'racing line'.
Obviously, this requires superb judgement to know when the apex of
the parabola has been reached – and as we will see later in this book,
even the best riders have been known to get it horribly wrong.

WAR OF WORDS

The birth of the Tour de France in 1903 can be reliably traced back to a bitter circulation war between two rival sporting newspapers in the 1890s. Le Vélo was the undisputed best-seller in France until a row between its owner and one of its main advertisers led to the establishment of L'Auto Vélo in 1899. Henri Desgrange, a 30-year-old former world hour-record holder, was hired as the new journal's editor. After a protracted legal wrangle, L'Auto was forced to drop Vélo from its masthead – but the ambitious Desgrange set about competing for its rival's circulation with a series of innovative stunts. One was to launch a cycle race around France, sponsored and organised – and of course covered in great detail – by L'Auto.

CIRCULATION IS THE MOTHER OF INVENTION

The idea for the Tour came not from Desgrange – although he would never seek to dispel the myth – but from his 23-year-old editorial assistant at *L'Auto,* Géo Lefèvre. Lefèvre himself never denied that he came up with the idea in desperation at a crisis meeting with Desgrange to discuss the plummeting circulation of the newspaper. At first Desgrange was not convinced. 'So what you are suggesting, petit Géo,' he said sniffily, 'is a Tour de France?' It was only when Victor Goddet, *L'Auto*'s financial manager, agreed to raid the company safe in order to fund the exercise that Desgrange changed his mind. Although Desgrange would later wax lyrical about the Tour, describing it as 'the great moral crusade of cycle sport', it's a fair assumption that if Goddet had said no, then the world's greatest cycle race would have been quietly shelved.

TOUR TRIVIA

Géo Lefèvre is also credited with having invented cyclo-cross, the branch of the sport in which cyclists follow a route that takes them off-road.

THE TOUR IS ON THE MENU

The historic meeting between Desgrange and Géo Lefèvre at which the idea for a round-France cycle race was first discussed took place at the Taverne Zimmer, a restaurant on the Boulevard de Montmartre in Paris. Although the venue is now the site of a TGI Friday, the occasion is marked by a small plaque on the wall.

ROLL UP FOR THE FIRST TOUR

The first Tour de France was grandly announced in *L'Auto* in January 1903 as a cycle race to cover 1,508 miles (2,428 km) in six stages between 31 May and 5 July, with no trainers or physios for the first five stages so that all riders would compete on equal terms.

When only fifteen riders had dared to register a week before the start date, Desgrange was forced to rethink. When he announced that the race was being extended from six to nineteen days, that the entry fee was being halved, and that expenses of five francs per day were to be paid to the first 50 finishers, the entries suddenly went up to 50.

TOUR TRIVIA

Belgian rider Julien Lootens rode the 1903 Tour under the pseudonym 'Samson'.

1903: GARIN SWEEPS TO VICTORY

At 3.16 pm on 31 May 1903, the first Tour de France set off from a small café named the Réveil Matin in the Parisian suburb of Villeneuve-St Georges. There were 50 riders from France, Belgium, Switzerland and Germany, 21 of whom were professionals – although such were the meagre wages for cyclists that none was full-time. When he was not in the saddle, the eventual winner, Maurice Garin – who stood just 5ft 3ins (160cm) tall – was a chimney sweep.

TOUR TRIVIA

For winning the first ever Tour de France, Garin was paid 3,000 francs. In modern money that works out at around €26,500 or £17,000.

ANATOMY OF A LEGEND: MAURICE GARIN

Garin was born in Arvier, Italy, in 1871, although he moved to France as a child.

He always rode in a fetching white jacket – an item of clothing that earned him the nickname 'The White Bulldog'. He was also known as the 'Little Chimney Sweep', because of the part-time job he did when he wasn't working in the family bike shop in Roubaix.

He was renowned for his long, droopy moustache and the cigarette hanging from the corner of his mouth.

Garin rode his first race in 1892, and two years later chalked up his first win: a 24-hour marathon staged around the streets of Liège.

6

After winning the first Tour de France, his adopted town of Lens organised a parade of honour for him.

Garin's brother César was also a Tour de France rider. The pair were among the top four riders disqualified for cheating in the 1904 Tour.

After retiring, Garin opened a garage and filling station on the main street in Lens, which he ran until his death in 1957.

TOUR TRIVIA

To distinguish him as the first leader of the race, Maurice Garin wore a green armband rather than the yellow jersey. This would not be introduced until 1919.

1903: THE FATHER OF THE FLOP?

Henri Desgrange is forever known as 'The Father of the Tour' – but in 1903 he was conspicuous by his absence from the start of the inaugural race. Indeed, as the 50 riders set off from the Parisian suburbs, Desgrange was back in his office in the city, evidently unwilling to associate himself with an event that could turn out to be a major flop. The only representative of *L'Auto* present at the *grand départ* was Desgrange's loyal assistant, Géo Lefèvre – the man who had first suggested the race to his boss eight years earlier.

1903: MARATHON ON WHEELS

The sheer length and winning times of the stages in the inaugural Tour de France in 1903 are eye-watering even to today's pro riders, who rarely ride more than 124 miles (200 km) in a day or spend more than

Vive le Tour!

six hours in the saddle.

Stage	From–To	Distance	Winner	Time
1:	Paris–Lyon,	290 miles (467 km)	Maurice Garin (FRA)	17h 45m
2:	Lyon–Marseilles	232 miles (374 km)	Hippolyte Acouturier (FRA)	14h 28m
3:	Marseilles–Toulouse	262 miles (423 km)	Hippolyte Acouturier (FRA)	17h 55m
4:	Toulouse–Bordeaux	166 miles (268 km)	Charles Laeser (SWI)	8h 46m
5:	Bordeaux–Nantes	264 miles (425 km)	Maurice Garin (FRA)	16h 26m
6:	Nantes–Paris	292 miles (471 km)	Maurice Garin (FRA)	18h 22m

RESULTS OF THE FIRST TOUR DE FRANCE

1st: Maurice Garin (France), 2,428 km in 94h 33m 14s (26.450 kph)
2nd: Lucien Pothier (France), + 2h 49m 21s
3rd: Fernand Augereau (France), + 4h 29m 24s
4th: Rodolfo Muller (Italy), + 4h 39m 30s
5th: Jean Fischer (France), + 4h 58m 44s
6th: Marcel Kerff (Belgium), + 5h 52m 24s
7th: Julien Lootens (Belgium), + 9h 31m 08s
8th: Georges Pasquier (France), + 10h 24m 04s
9th: François Beaugendre (France), + 10h 52m 14s
10th: Aloîs Catteau (Belgium), + 12h 44m 57s

1903: SURVIVAL OF THE FITTEST

Although 50 riders started the Tour, only 21 survived the 1,508 miles (2,428 km) marathon. The last man to finish was Frenchman Arsène Millocheau, in a time of 159h 27m – a full two days behind Maurice Garin. The first riders to sign on for the race way back at the Réveil

Matin bar, Henri Ellinamour and Léon Pernette, had simply disappeared during the course of the race.

1903: LAP OF HONOUR

The inaugural Tour finished with a circuit of the newly built concrete cycle track at the Parc des Princes in Paris. A crowd of 20,000 was waiting to greet the riders as they arrived, although an estimated 100,000 spectators lined the route through the suburbs of Paris.

Vive le Tour!

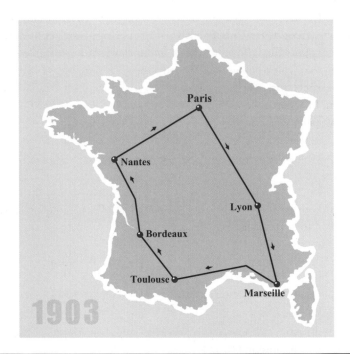

1903: A HIT WITH THE READERS

Any doubts Henri Desgrange may have had about the popularity of the Tour were dispelled by the circulation figures of *L'Auto* during the nineteen days of the inaugural race, as it showed daily sales of 65,000 (up from 30,000). A special edition of the journal, produced within minutes of the race ending in Paris, sold over 130,000 copies.

1903: HIPPO SPIKED

Maurice Garin's main rival for the 1903 Tour was fellow countryman Hippolyte Acouturier. Suspiciously – or perhaps not, considering Garin's exploits the following year – Acouturier failed to complete the first stage to Lyon when he was handed a drink of spiked lemonade by a roadside spectator, which turned his legs to jelly and forced him to abandon. In accordance with the rules, Acouturier rejoined the race for the next stage, which he duly won along with the third. However, Garin was unconcerned because having abandoned the first stage, Acouturier was no longer in contention for the overall classification.

'We are satisfied, for this year we have given cycle-sport its finest, its greatest competitive event at a time when know-alls were saying it was impossible to better what was already on offer.'

Henri Desgrange, 1903

'The Tour is finished and I am very afraid that its second edition will be its last. It will have been killed by its own success, driven out of control by blind passion, by violence and filthy suspicions worthy only of ignorant and dishonourable men.'

Henri Desgrange, 1904

1904: CHEATING AND SKULDUGGERY

The cheating scandals that have marred the history of the Tour de France are generally thought to be a modern phenomenon. The Tour, however, was mired in controversy as early as its second year.

In July 1904, Maurice Garin cruised to what appeared to be a second consecutive victory. Four months later, however, he, along with the next three riders in the General Classification, were stripped of their places by the organisers and thrown out of the Tour after investigations revealed a catalogue of skulduggery on the back roads to Paris.

These included itching powder in riders' shorts, spiked drinks, sabotaged bike frames, and nails and broken glass scattered across the road. Race favourite Hippolyte Acouturier, himself a victim of a spiked drink in 1903, was spotted taking a tow from a car by means of a string attached to a cork which he gripped between his teeth. Garin bribed Géo Lefèvre to give him an illegal feed. He and rival Pierre Chevallier were also rumoured to have made up lost time by getting a lift in a car when darkness fell. And all this was just on stage one!

The next stage nearly ended in anarchy on the slopes of the Col de la République when a hundred supporters of local rider Antoine Faure blocked the road and set about the riders with cudgels while their man sped off up the road. The mob dispersed only when Lefèvre fired his revolver into the air.

Things got worse on stage three, when more than 2,000 locals fought with police, officials and riders in Nîmes after their favourite was disqualified for slipstreaming a car. This time it was Lefèvre's colleague Jean Miral who had to fire the warning shot.

As well as being stripped of his win, Garin was banned for two years. Chevalier was banned for life, while others such as Acouturier escaped with fines and reprimands. Fifth-placed Henri Cornet, despite being warned about his conduct, was declared the overall winner.

It was a scandal that threatened to strangle the Tour at birth. However, it also set a precedent for uncompromising action by the organisers against cheats, evident in the Festina Affair of 1998 (see The Festina Affair, page 210) and the mass expulsions on the eve of the 2006 Tour (see 2006: Operation Puerto, page 245).

Garin, meanwhile, continued to protest his innocence until shortly before his death in 1957, aged 85. In his later years, when asked if he had cheated, he would simply shrug his shoulders and say, 'I was young'.

TOUR TRIVIA
Henri Cornet and Lucien Petit-Breton are the only riders to have won the Tour de France under false names.

'If I'm not murdered before Paris, I'll win the Tour again.'

> **Maurice Garin**, who survived to win his
> second Tour, before being expelled for cheating

TOUR TRIVIA
Up until the 1950s, riders used to carry up to three spare tyres looped around their shoulders in case of puncture.

TOUR TRIVIA
At 19 years and 11 months, Henri Cornet is the youngest winner of the Tour de France – even if it was by default. The oldest is Fermin Lambot of Belgium, who was 37 years old when he won in 1922.

Anquetil   Merckx   Hinault

Indurain   Armstrong

THE ALL TIME GREATS

Jacques Anquetil, Eddy Merckx, Bernard Hinault and Miguel Indurain all won the Tour five times. The American Lance Armstrong won it an unprecedented seven.

1905: THE CHEATING CONTINUES

Despite the punitive steps taken by Tour organisers in the wake of the 1904 race, cheating was still up and running in 1905. An estimated 56 lb (125 kg) of nails were scattered across the road to Nancy during the first stage, resulting in only fifteen finishers out of a field of 60. Initially, Henri Desgrange wanted to cancel the race, but he eventually relented and allowed any rider who had finished the stage by car or train to rejoin the Tour for the next stage.

TOUR TRIVIA

For winning the 1905 Tour, Louis Trousselier was awarded the princely sum of 6,950 francs. He promptly lost the lot in a card game.

1906: POTTIER SOARS

In 1905 René Pottier amazed everyone by climbing the murderous ascent of the Ballon d'Alsace without once dismounting and at an average speed of 12 mph (20 kph). The following year, he destroyed the field by winning five of the thirteen stages and with it the race. Desgrange was delighted. After two years of scandal, here at last was a worthy winner of the Tour. Unfortunately, Pottier, wracked with depressive illness, killed himself just six months later at the age of 29. He was found hanged from the hook on which he kept his bicycle.

1907: LITTLE BRETON PROVES TO BE A BIG WINNER

The 1907 Tour winner was Lucien Petit-Breton. As with many cyclists of that era, it was not the name he was born with. In fact, Lucien Mazan earned his soubriquet as a boy in Buenos Aires, where his family had emigrated at the end of the nineteenth century. His family disapproved of cycling, so on his return to France, Mazan used his nickname instead.

1907: LUCKY LUCIEN

Petit-Breton's win was undoubtedly fortunate. When runaway race leader Émile Georget was relegated to last place and fined 550 francs for using a series of unauthorised bikes, many of the riders quit the race in protest that the punishment wasn't hard enough. That left Petit-Breton, until then out of contention, a clear run to Paris for the victory.

TOUR TRIVIA
Alfred Le Bars cycled to the start of the 1907 Tour from his home in Morlaix – a mere 310 miles (500 km). It took him nearly 19 hours. Four kilometres into the race, he crashed and had to borrow a spectator's bike. However, he somehow managed to finish 26th overall – out of 33 riders.

1908: DOUBLE TOP FOR PETIT-BRETON

By winning in 1908, Lucien Petit-Breton became the first man to win back-to-back Tours. It was a slap in the face for those critics who suggested his win the previous year had been something of a fluke.

TOUR TRIVIA
The Champs Élysées in Paris first became part of the Tour in 1908 when it was used as the start of the race. It wasn't used as a regular finishing point until 1975, when Walter Godefroot beat Rik van Linden in a sprint.

TOUR TRIVIA
Georges Goffin of Belgium started three Tours, in 1909, 1911 and 1922 – and abandoned them all on the first day.

1909: A GIANT WIN FOR LUXEMBOURG

In 1909 François Faber of Luxembourg not only became the first man to win five consecutive stages, but was also the first non-French rider to win the Tour. It was no mean achievement for a giant of a man who stood 6 ft (183 cm) tall and weighed a massive 14st 3lb (91kg). Compare that to the modern Tour rider, who would regard himself as overweight if he tipped the scales at 11 stone (75 kg); Magnus Backstedt, the Swede currently reckoned to be the heaviest in the pro tour, weighs 14 stone (90 kg). Despite being from Luxembourg, Faber was a great hero among the French fans. More than 20,000 of them waited to see him finish the stage into Lyon, and the Parc des Princes was full as he arrived to claim his one and only Tour win. As he entered the stadium, his chain broke and Faber was forced to run more than a kilometre to the finish line – the equivalent of a lap of honour.

TOUR TRIVIA
During the 1909 Tour, Henri Alavoine of France crashed in horrendous snow, hail and freezing rain and was forced to carry his bike through freezing ankle-high water to the stage finish some 6 miles (10 km) away.

1910: ASSASSINS!

On a warm July day Henri Desgrange received a telegram from Alphonse Steines, one of his minions who had been sent to check on conditions at the top of the Col du Tourmalet in the Pyrenees. 'Have crossed the Tourmalet on foot Stop,' it read. 'Road passable to vehicles Stop No snow Stop.'

Desgrange was overjoyed. Sending the riders up the Pyrenean giant was a stunt he had been considering for some time; one he knew would increase circulation of *L'Auto*. But Steines, no doubt terrified of incurring the wrath of his boss, had lied. By the time the lead riders reached the top of the mountain, they had been forced to trudge through deep snow drifts, mud and sub-zero temperatures. As Octave Lapize, the eventual race winner, staggered to the summit of the next mountain on the route, the Aubisque, he glared at the waiting Tour officials and hissed the words '*Vous êtes des assassins!*'

910: DEATH BY JELLYFISH

Despite perilous descents, murderous stages and bikes that had a tendency to fall apart, the first Tour fatality occurred on a rest day. Adolphe Hélière was bathing in the sea off Nice when he suffered heart failure after being stung by a jellyfish.

'Anyway, you can see that I haven't lost too much weight: look, my detachable collars are still a perfect fit! That was my only real worry — to have to go out and buy some smaller ones.'

> **Octave Lapize** laughs off the hardships required to win the
> 2,943 mile (4,473 km) Tour of 1910

910: DESGRANGE STAMPS HIS AUTHORITY

Henri Desgrange went to some extraordinary lengths to ensure his precious Tour was not open to cheating. One such step was to insist that each rider's bike was taken to the offices of *L'Auto* in Paris, where the pedals and fork-head were stamped with an official hallmark. As if this wasn't enough, the bikes were also fitted with an invisible stamp so they could not be changed during the race.

1910: ALL ABOARD THE BROOM WAGON

The broom wagon – or *la voiture balai* – was first introduced in 1910. As its name suggests, the purpose of this vehicle is to 'sweep up' riders at the back of the field who can no longer continue or simply wish to retire from the race. Their numbers are unceremoniously removed and they are bundled in to the back. Star riders rarely use the broom wagon, preferring the less inauspicious option of climbing into the back of their team cars.

LEGENDARY MOUNTAINS OF THE TOUR: COL DU GALIBIER

After sending the Tour through the Pyrenees in 1910, Desgrange decided to up the stakes the following year by devising a route through the Alps. This included the fearsome Col du Galibier, which at 8,386 ft (2,556 m) was the highest point yet attempted by the Tour. Émile Georget was the first rider to cross the summit. Although it was 12 July, the Galibier was still covered in snow, and the road – if that is indeed what it can be called – was a quagmire of mud and gravel used only by loggers and smugglers. At the end of the stage, Georget – looking like some sort of soaking wet mud-monster – climbed wearily off his bike, approached a startled official, and said: 'That's given you something to think about.'

Vive le Tour!

'We had to cross the Galibier. The stage start was amusing: downhill all the way! But soon the fun began, and by fun I refer to the tasteless prank of slipping mountains under the roads of our beautiful country!'

Gustave Garrigou, winner of the 1911 Tour

1911: CHRISTOPHE GOES FOR BROKE

The 1911 Tour featured its longest-ever break when Eugène Christophe stayed clear of the pack for 195 miles (315 km) of the 200 mile (323 km) stage between Chamonix and Grenoble.

TOUR TRIVIA

Touristes-routiers were amateurs who were allowed to enter the Tour as long as they made their own travel and accommodation arrangements. One of the most famous was Jules Deloffre, who would perform acrobatic tricks in the market square after a stage in order to raise money for bed and board that night. He appeared in no fewer than fifteen Tours between 1908 and 1928, completing seven and finishing as high as fifteenth on two occasions. The last *touristes-routiers* competed in the 1938 Tour.

1912: AN UDDERLY UNFORTUNATE ACCIDENT

Lucien Petit-Breton won the Tour in style in 1908 — but four years later he was forced to withdraw from the race after a decidedly embarrassing collision with a cow. A year earlier he had the equal misfortune to hit a drunken sailor attempting to cross the road in downtown Boulogne.

TOUR TRIVIA

In 1913, the Tour set off around France in an anti-clockwise direction for the first time. Since then the direction of the race has alternated each year.

LEGENDARY MOUNTAINS OF THE TOUR: BALLON D'ALSACE

The Ballon d'Alsace was the first mountain introduced to the Tour in 1905. It stands at 4,091 ft (1,247 m), and as he announced it, Henri Desgrange confidently predicted that no one would ever be able to ride it. As he drove to the summit to await the stragglers, it must have come as a shock to Desgrange to be overtaken by René Pottier on his bike.

TOUR TRIVIA

In 1913 the Tour changed from points to times as a means of deciding the winner.

1913: F****** FORKS!

The idea of support cars carrying replacement bicycles was unheard of in the early years of the Tour. In fact, riders faced severe time penalties if they caught receiving any help at all to effect mechanical repairs. It was this typically draconian rule that led to an incident which has gone down in Tour legend.

While descending the Col du Tourmalet at high speed, Eugène Christophe's front forks snapped. Remarkably, he was unscathed. Even more remarkably, Christophe – aware that he was the race leader on the road – slung his bike over his shoulder, grabbed the remains of the forks, and set off on foot for the nearest village 6 miles (10 km) further down the mountain. The village was St Marie de Campan, and right in the middle of it was a blacksmith. Stoking up the forge, Christophe set about repairing his forks. As he did so, an eagle-eyed Tour official looked on to ensure that no rules were broken. When Christophe asked a local youngster to work the bellows, he was informed by the official that he had been docked ten minutes – on top of the four hours he had already lost since the crash.

Such was the outcry over the decision, the time penalty was eventually reduced – to three minutes. By then, though, Christophe was already well out of the reckoning.

Towards the end of his life, Christophe returned to St Marie de Campan to watch the unveiling of a commemorative plaque on the site of the former smithy. To add insult to injury, the Tour organisers spelled his name wrong.

1913: THE TOUR OF WINNERS

There were no fewer than ten past or future Tour winners contesting the 1913 Tour: Louis Trousselier (1905), Lucien Petit-Breton (1907 and 1908), François Faber (1909), Octave Lapize (1910), Gustave Garrigou (1911), Odile Defraye (1912), Philippe Thys (1913, 1914 and 1920), Firmin Lambot (1919 and 1922), Léon Scieur (1921) and Henri Pélissier (1923).

TOUR TRIVIA
Eighteen-year-old Tunisian rider Ali Neffati rode the 1913 Tour wearing a fez.

TOUR TRIVIA

Don Kirkham and Ivor Munro became the first Australians to take part in the Tour when they entered the race in 1914.

1914: A SHOT THAT WAS HEARD AROUND THE WORLD

At three in the morning of 28 June 1914 in Paris, Henri Desgrange fired the starting pistol to begin the eleventh Tour de France. A few hours later, in Sarajevo, a Serbian nationalist called Gavrilo Princip fired the shots that killed Archduke Franz Ferdinand and his wife Sophie, an act which precipitated World War One.

☆ TOUR STARS WHO WERE KILLED IN THE GREAT WAR

Lucien Petit-Breton, aged 25: winner 1907 and 1908

François Faber, aged 28: winner 1909

Octave Lapize, aged 30: winner 1910

Émile Engel, aged 23: winner of the first stage of the 1914 race

François Lafourcade, aged 36: first man to cross the summit of the Col d'Aubisque in 1910

☆ TOUR STARS BORN IN 1914

Gino Bartali: The great pre-war Italian cyclist, known as *Il Pio* (The Pious) because of his deep religious convictions. A great rival of fellow countryman Fausto Coppi, he competed in eight Tours between 1937 and 1953, winning in 1938 and 1948 and finishing second in 1949.

TOUR WINNERS 1903–1914

1903: Maurice Garin (FRA)
1904: Henri Cornet (FRA)
1905: Louis Trousselier (FRA)
1906: René Poitier (FRA)
1907: Lucien Petit-Breton (FRA)
1908: Lucien Petit-Breton (FRA)
1909: François Faber (LUX)
1910: Octave Lapize (FRA)
1911: Gustave Garrigou (FRA)
1912: Odiel Defraye (BEL)
1913: Philippe Thys (BEL)
1914: Philippe Thys (BEL)

NEW IDEAS AND BOLD INITIATIVES 1919–1939

'What can be done to haul cycling out of its rut of tedium? New ideas! Bold initiatives!'

L'Equipe

1919: TOUR OF HOPE

The Tour of this year was, understandably, a sombre affair. Three of its past winners were dead and the race travelled through a country ravaged by four years of ruinous war. Due to the scarcity of raw materials, cycle manufacturers were forced to pool their resources in order to ensure the riders actually had bike frames, tyres, brakes and gears.

But in many ways the Tour was precisely what the French people needed after so long in the dark, and they turned out in their hundreds of thousands to line the route and cheer on their favourites. And of all the riders there was no one they loved more than Eugène Christophe. The man whose broken forks had cost him victory in the 1913 Tour was back, and for thirteen stages he dominated the race. By the time the peloton set off on the penultimate stage – a monstrous 290 miles (468 km) between Metz and Dunkirk – Christophe was 30 minutes ahead of his nearest challenger, Firmin Lambot. But then, astonishingly, his forks broke again, and by the time he had repaired them he was two and a half hours behind the bemused Lambot. In a rare act of compassion, Henri Desgrange organised a subscription in *L'Auto* in which readers were asked to contribute to a compensation fund for the hapless rider. The subscription raised 13,000 francs – far more than Christophe would have ever won as a Tour winner. Like Raymond Poulidor in the 1960s, Christophe would never win the Tour; but like the legendary Pou-Pou he became more famous and beloved as the eternal second as any winner would ever be.

TOUR TRIVIA

Today, tyre punctures are easily fixed, but in the early years of the Tour the only way to patch a leaky inner-tube was to cut through the tyre, which then had to be sewn back together with twine and a sailmaker's needle.

1919: THE FIRST TIME IN YELLOW

There was a somewhat brighter postscript to Eugène Christophe's catastrophic Tour. At the beginning of stage eleven from Grenoble to Geneva, Henri Desgrange presented him with a yellow jersey designed to identify him as the race leader. Christophe, though he never won it outright, therefore became the first rider to wear the legendary *maillot jaune* of the Tour de France. Unfortunately for Christophe, the jersey made him a laughing stock: all along the route, spectators called him a 'canary'.

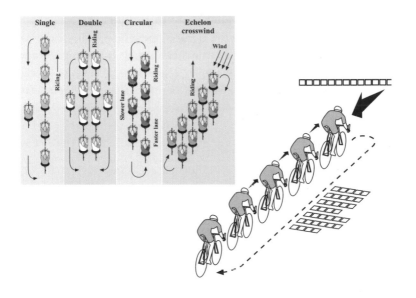

TOUR TRIVIA

Fermin Lambot always rode with 500 francs in his back pocket, in case his bike broke and he had to buy a new one.

▲ LEGENDARY MOUNTAINS OF THE TOUR: COL D'AUBISQUE

With a summit at 5,607 ft (1,709 m) the Aubisque is one of the beasts of the Pyrenees. It was first introduced into the Tour in 1910, when the organisers paid 20,000 francs to repair the road, and the first man to its snow-covered summit on 21 July was François Lafourcade. Next over was Octave Lapize, who uttered the immortal words '*Vous-êtes des assassins!'* at the waiting Tour organisers. While the climb to the summit is not regarded as demanding – the average gradient is 8 per cent at the top – the descent is perilous, with narrow roads, hairpin bends and gradients that can reach 13 per cent. It was on the descent of the Aubisque that Dutchman Wim van Est went headfirst into a ravine and had to be pulled to safety by means of knotted inner tubes (see Wrong Turn for Wim, page 76).

1919: FIT TO DROP

After four years of war and privation, fitness levels were understandably low among riders in the 1919 Tour – which explains why the average winning speed of just 14.9 mph (24 kph) was the slowest in Tour history, and why out of 130 riders just ten made it to Paris.

TOUR TRIVIA

The whopping 299 mile (482 km) stage from Les Sables d'Olonne to Bayonne in 1919 was the longest in Tour history. Riders breathed a sigh of relief when it was finally discontinued in 1924.

1920: UNLUCKY EUGÈNE – AGAIN!

Philippe Thys, the great Belgian rider, became the first man to win three Tours when he triumphed in 1920. As in 1913, his main rival was Eugène Christophe, and as ever Christophe would be dogged by bad luck. This time, severe back pain forced the veteran Frenchman to withdraw. It was a year dominated by Belgians, however. As well as

Thys, who won four stages and never finished outside the top five in any stage, Belgians won twelve out of the fifteen stages and took the first seven places in the overall classification. The best-placed Frenchman was eighth – and Honoré Barthélémy staggered over the line with a broken wrist and a dislocated collarbone after a crash on the final stage.

ANATOMY OF A LEGEND: PHILIPPE THYS

Thys was born in Anderlecht, Belgium, in 1890 and was the first rider to win three Tours. He died, aged 80, in 1971.

He would also have been the first man to wear the yellow jersey, had he accepted Henri Desgrange's offer. Instead he rejected it, claiming it would make him more visible to his rivals on the road. This was in 1913 – six years before Eugène Christophe first wore the *maillot jaune*.

Thys won his second Tour in 1914. When the race resumed in 1919, he was so fat and slow that Desgrange accused him of being arrogant and a disgrace both to himself and the sport of cycling. Stung, Thys duly lost weight, trained like a madman, and won the 1920 Tour by 57 minutes.

1920: NAPOLEON BLOWNAPART

In the history of the Tour can there ever have been an unluckier rider than the Italian Napoleon Paoli? While racing down a narrow mountain track, he collided with a donkey that was standing in the middle of the road. Both he and his bike flew into the air and, when he landed, Paoli was on the back of the donkey. The beast of burden duly set off in panic in the opposite direction, with the helpless Paoli unable to get off. When the donkey eventually collapsed from exhaustion, Paoli had to run nearly a kilometre to where his bike was lying by the roadside. But that was not the end of his travails. Further along the road, he was hit on the head by a rock that had worked loose from an overhanging cliff. Dazed and confused, Paoli managed to get to the summit of the Tourmalet, where he gave up and fell asleep in a hut. In all he would ride three Tours, and finish none of them.

1921: DAYTRIPPERS

In cycling there are Stars, there are Water Carriers – and there are those who simply hang on for grim death and hope to finish the race in one piece. One can only feel sorry for poor Henri Miège, a French amateur, who set out on the 241 mile (388 km) first stage of the 1921 Tour full of high hopes, only to wobble over the line in Le Havre 24 hours later and fully nine hours behind the race leader. But this was a daytrip compared to the travails of Laurent Devalle of Monaco, who took more than 27 hours to complete the 299 mile (482 km) stage from Les Sables d'Olonne to Bayonne four days later.

TOUR TRIVIA

Romain Bellenger of France abandoned the 1921 Tour after drinking water from a mountain spring. The freezing water caused cramps and diarrhoea.

1922: OLDIE BUT A GOODIE

Firmin Lambot's win in the 1922 Tour at the age of 37 was the first by a rider who didn't win a stage of the race. He also became the oldest winner of the Tour.

1922: 'TWO-BIKES' GRASSIN

Henri Desgrange was a stickler for the rules, especially if it ensured maximum discomfort for his riders. He would have been pleased, then, in 1922, when Frenchman Robert Grassin broke a fork just 40 miles (65 km) into the mammoth 226 mile (364 km) stage between Le Havre and Cherbourg. According to the rules, riders had to complete the race on, or with, their own bikes. Consequently, Grassin – after spending three hours in a failed attempt to repair his bike – was forced to borrow a spare and complete the remaining 186 miles (300 km) with the broken bike over his shoulder. His point made, Grassin unsurprisingly quit the race in disgust the following day and never rode the Tour again

TOUR TRIVIA
The 1922 Tour included for the first time the climbs of the Col de Vars and the Col d'Izoard.

1923: DESGRANGE EATS HIS WORDS

Henri Desgrange and leading French rider Henri Pélissier never got on. There was something about Pélissier's laid-back, almost disrespectful style that got right up the Father of the Tour's nose. Indeed in 1921, Desgrange wrote, 'This Pélissier does not know how to suffer. He will never win the Tour de France.' Two years later, Pélissier made Desgrange eat his words with a superlative display of aggressive riding in the Alps which salvaged a 30 minute deficit and turned it into a 30 minute winning margin.

Desgrange was not averse to the odd piece of purple prose, as we have seen, and at the end of the race he was describing how: 'The mountains seemed to sink lower, sunk by the victorious thrust of his muscle. More than a score of times on the most vicious gradients, hands on the tops of the bars, he looked down at the valley bottoms, like an eagle staring at his prey.'

TOUR TRIVIA

The 1923 Tour was the first in which time bonuses were awarded to stage winners – two minutes per stage.

ANATOMY OF A LEGEND: OTTAVIO BOTTECCHIA

In 1923 Ottavio Bottecchia became the first Italian to wear the yellow jersey when he won the 230 mile (371 km) second stage from Le Havre to Cherbourg. He clearly enjoyed the experience because the following year he became the first rider to wear it from start to finish.

Bottecchia was born in 1894 in the village of San Martino di Colle Umberto near Treviso, and worked as a bricklayer before joining the Italian army in 1914, where he served as a sharpshooter. He was captured shortly before the end of the war, but escaped.

His cycling exploits made him the first of a line of great Italian cyclists including Alfredo Binda, Constante Girardengo, Gino Bartali and Fausto Coppi – but despite winning back-to-back Tours in 1923 and 1924, he was never as popular in Italy as he should have been.

Today he is best remembered for the circumstances of his mysterious and violent death in 1927. In June of that year he was found by the roadside near his home with serious head injuries. At first it was assumed he'd had a crash, yet his bike was undamaged and propped up against a tree. An official inquiry concluded it was an accident – although many people suspected that the proudly socialist Bottecchia had fallen foul of Fascist mobsters. Two people later confessed to killing him: a farmer who accused him of stealing grapes, and a dying New York Italian gangster who claimed he'd done the job under contract. But to this day nobody is quite sure just how – or why – the first great Italian Tour champion met his bloody end.

'It would be dangerous to follow Bottecchia up a mountain pass. In fact it would be suicidal. His progression is so powerful and regular that we would be asphyxiated.'

Nicolas Frantz, Tour winner

'If I'm going well, my tyres burst. If my tyres don't burst I feel like I'm the one who's breathing my last!'

Jean Alavoine after finishing fourteenth in the 1924 Tour

1924: THE TOUR OF SUFFERING

The 1924 Tour was dubbed '*Le Tour du Souffrance*' (The Tour of Suffering) by journalist Alfred Londres, and there is little doubt that in terms of draconian rules and regulations, Henri Desgrange excelled himself this year. Not content with forcing riders to contest fifteen stages in which only two were under 186 miles (300 km) and five were in excess of 248 miles (400 km), and insisting that they had no mechanical back-up, Desgrange decided that in addition, riders would be disqualified if they were found to be discarding clothing or equipment on route. When most stages started in the pre-dawn cold and finished in the burning afternoon heat, this was perhaps the greatest torture of all. It proved too much for Henri Pélissier, who withdrew from the race claiming that Desgrange would soon insist on riders carrying weights 'since God made humans too light'.

TOUR TRIVIA
Jules Banino of France was 51 when he rode the Tour for the second and last time in 1924 – the oldest man to compete in the world's toughest sporting event.

1925: THE END OF AN ERA

The 1925 Tour marked the end of an era with the retirement of Eugène Christophe, nineteen years after he first competed in the event. It was also the last Tour for the three-times Belgian winner Philippe Thys and, no doubt to Henri Desgrange's great relief, the maverick Henri Pélissier.

TEAM SPORT

Tours in this era were, for the first time, centred around sponsored teams rather than a collection of individuals. The two dominant outfits were Automoto-Hutchinson, which boasted stars like Thys, Pélissier and Bottecchia, and Alcyon-Dunlop, which featured up-and-coming riders such as Nicolas Frantz and Louis Mottiat. Other teams included Louvet-Pouchois, Thomann-Dunlop, Armor-Dunlop, Christophe-Hutchinson and Météor-Wolber.

TOUR TRIVIA

The often inhuman conditions Tour riders were expected to endure were revealed in an article written by the French journalist Albert Londres. Fittingly, it was entitled *Les Forçats de la Route* (Convicts of the Road).

1925: A WIN FOR MY DAUGHTER

At the ripe old age of 32, Lucien Buysse of Belgium won the Tour of 1925. He did so despite the news that his daughter, one of four children, had died during the race. Buysse, distraught, was ready to abandon and go home. But his family urged him to continue, and continue he did, arriving in Paris a full 1 hour 28 minutes ahead of Nicolas Frantz of Luxembourg. Weeping, he raised his hands to the heavens and exclaimed, 'I thought of you during all the hardest hours of the race.'

1926: CIRCLE OF DEATH

The 1926 Tour – the longest ever at 3,569 miles (5,745 km) – was pretty much anybody's race until it was blown apart in the cataclysmic tenth stage between Bayonne and Luchon. This was a 200 mile (323 km) slog around the so-called 'Circle of Death', which included the Pyrenean monsters Osquich, Aubisque, Soulor, Tourmalet, Aspin and Peyresourde. In 1913, Philippe Thys had won the same stage in under fourteen hours. But that day the sun had been shining. Thirteen years later, the riders were faced with snow, rain, fog and bitter cold. At six o'clock, when Lucien Buysse eventually staggered over the line in first place, he had been in the saddle for over seventeen hours. An hour later, only ten more riders had appeared from the murk and by midnight there were a paltry 54. With 22 riders still unaccounted for, even Desgrange began to worry and despatched rescue cars to find them. They were found sheltering in houses and bars all the way back to Bayonne. Although they were subsequently transported back to Luchon, Desgrange deemed that they were all out of the race – which more or less gave victory to Buysse.

1926: FRENCH FARCE

There were no French stage winners in 1926, something which had never happened before and would not happen again for another 73 years.

'You have no idea what the Tour de France is. It's Calvary. But do you want to see how we keep going? Cocaine for our eyes and chloroform for our gums. Have you seen us in the bath at the finish? Take away the mud and we're as white as shrouds. Diarrhoea empties us. In the evenings, in our rooms, we dance a jig like St Vitus instead of sleeping. Think what happens to our skin and the nails of our feet. I've lost six out of ten. They fall off little by little every stage.'

Henri Pélissier describes the hardship of the Tour de France

LEGENDARY MOUNTAINS OF THE TOUR: COL DE LA MADELEINE

A beast of an Alp, the Col de la Madeleine rises savagely from 1,673 ft (510 m) to 6,509 ft (1,984 m) in a little over 23 miles (38 km), at a gradient of 9 per cent. This is bad enough ascending, but coming down the mountain can be perilous. In 1983 Dutch rider Johan van der Velde skidded on a hairpin bend and went over the edge. Miraculously, he landed on a ledge just a few feet below and was able to climb back up. The Madeleine was first included in the Tour in 1969, when Spanish rider Andres Gandarias was the first rider over the summit.

TOUR TRIVIA
Kisso Kawamuro became the first Japanese rider to compete in the Tour in 1926.

1926: EH?-VIAN

Evian is a small town in the east of France — but that was news to most of the peloton who lined up for the 1926 Tour. In fact, so few of them knew the location of the first-ever *Grand Départ* outside Paris that they had to be taken there by train.

1927: BACK TO THE DRAWING BOARD

Having clamped down on cheating, divided the field into amateurs and professionals, and added what he thought were eye-catching stages in the Alps and Pyrenees, Desgrange was perturbed to discover from his stagnating circulation figures that the French love affair with *le Tour* was waning.

The reason for this was two-fold: first, there was a distinct lack of competitive French riders, and much as they liked cycling, it was galling for Frenchmen to read about their great race being dominated by Belgians and Luxemburgers.

Secondly, the leading professional teams had the event in a stranglehold. Apart from the mountain stages – when the conditions meant anything could happen – the race had become yawn-inducingly predictable on the flat. Teams would protect their star riders to the extent that by the time they reached the mountains, the likes of Nicolas Frantz (Alcyon-Dunlop) and Maurice Dewaele (Labor-Dunlop) had barely broken sweat. While Desgrange could do little about the first problem other than pray for the arrival of the next Maurice Garin (or even the much-loathed Henri Pélissier), in 1927 he took typically forthright steps to generate more interest in the interim stages between the mountains. This took the form of team time trials. Desgrange's theory was that if the teams didn't know what the others were doing, they would have no alternative but to ride flat out.

Time trials were held for the first nine stages, and when Francis Pélissier – a Frenchman, no less! – led the unfancied Dilecta-Wolber team to victory in stage one between Paris and Dieppe, the idea appeared to be working. Pélissier wore yellow for four more stages, but a more open Tour proved to be an illusion. For a start, had they not suffered more than twenty punctures on the first stage, Frantz's all-powerful

Alcyon team would have won by a mile. As it was, by the time the Tour entered the Pyrenees on stage eleven, Frantz was perfectly placed to strike. This he did, to the usual devastating effect. Indeed, by the time the race left the Pyrenees, Frantz had a huge lead over the rest of the field, and his winning margin in Paris was the biggest for fifteen years.

It was back to the drawing board for Desgrange – although there was one distant ray of hope on the horizon. The 1927 Tour saw the debuts of Antonin Magne and André Leducq, two French riders who would come to dominate the race in the 1930s.

TOUR TRIVIA

French rider Ferdinand le Drogo wore the yellow jersey for just one day in 1927 – but it happened to be the day the Tour passed through his home town. Satisfied that he had made himself a local hero, le Drogo quit the race the next day.

1927: TOUR DOMINATION

If Desgrange's cunning plan to open up the Tour look fatally holed beneath the waterline in 1927, it was blown completely out of the water the following year. Not only did Nicolas Frantz win the race, he wore yellow from stage one, and second and third positions were both taken by Alcyon riders. To rub salt into the wound, Frantz completed the nineteenth stage between Metz and Charleville on a woman's bike borrowed from a cycle shop, as his own had broken with 60 miles (100 km) to go.

928: TOUR DOWN UNDER

The Tour went truly international for the first time in 1928 when a combined Australian/New Zealand team competed. Team leader Hubert Opperman finished a highly creditable eighteenth.

☆ TOUR STARS BORN IN 1928

Federico Bahamontés: The superlative Spanish climber, known as the Eagle of Toledo, who competed in ten Tours between 1954 and 1965, winning one and finishing as King of the Mountains, having achieved the most accumulated points in the mountain stages, in six.

929: MORE F****** FORKS!

In 1913 Eugène Christophe's valiant attempts to repair his broken bike at a village blacksmith became the stuff of tour legend. By 1929, however, Desgrange's steadfast refusal to allow replacement bikes was the subject of much dark muttering among Tour riders and observers. The man who sparked the controversy this year was Frenchman Victor Fontan. Leading by a race-winning ten minutes in the Pyrenees, Fontan was halfway through a tricky descent when, like Christophe, his forks broke. Unlike Christophe, the nearest village did not have a blacksmith. Fontan is reputed to have knocked on every door, pleading to borrow a replacement bike. No sooner had he set off, than he punctured. With his Tour over, Fontan climbed off and sobbed by the roadside. It was the first and last time he would wear the coveted yellow jersey.

'How can a man lose the Tour de France because of an accident to his bike? The rules should provide for a back-up vehicle with spare bikes on board. You lose the Tour to a better rider; you should not lose it because of a stupid accident to your bike!'

Louis Delblat, journalist, after runaway 1929 Tour leader Victor Fontan was forced to retire after his bike hit a pothole in the Pyrenees

1929: NO SYMPATHY

Although it had been split into 24 stages, with only four over 186 miles (300 km), the Tour remained a savage test of endurance. In 1929, the great Belgian Maurice Dewaele, wearing yellow after Fontan's unfortunate withdrawal, was so drained by the Pyrenees that he collapsed at the start line of stage eleven and had to be held up on his bike by two team-mates for the first few kilometres. Remarkably, Dewaele clung on to yellow all the way to Paris – but inevitably Henri Desgrange was not impressed.

'How can such a soft touch retain the yellow jersey?' he demanded. 'Why didn't his rivals attack him more resolutely? What can one make of their tactics and the real worth of the winner? I declare the winner moribund!'

☆ TOUR STARS BORN IN 1929

André Darrigade: He competed in fourteen Tours between 1953 and 1966, and was during that time the event's pre-eminent sprinter. Indeed, Darrigade holds the record for the greatest number of wins on the first stage, grabbing the yellow jersey five times. In all, he won sixteen yellow jerseys and 22 stages. Only Eddy Merckx (34), Bernard Hinault (28) and André Leducq (25) have won more.

1930: THE GRAVY TRAIN

The Tour de France publicity caravan was devised in 1930 as a means of raising money for the event without having to rely on the major bike manufacturers, whose influence was slowly killing the Tour. Back then it consisted of a few advertising vehicles chugging along in the riders' wake. Today, there are more than 200, and the caravan is an event in itself. It sets off two hours before the riders and stretches fully 15 miles (25 km) along the route, showering spectators with cheap giveaways.

1930: NATIONAL PRIDE

Desgrange may have dismissed Tour winner Maurice Dewaele as 'moribund', but he knew full well that the Tour itself was on its last legs. 1930 saw yet another attempt to breathe new life into the event, this time with the introduction of national teams instead of manufacturers' outfits. France, Belgium, Germany, Spain and Italy each entered teams of eight riders, with the rest of the 100-strong field made up of amateurs. Whether this increased excitement is debatable – but it certainly had the effect of creating French domination, with Andre Leducq winning the race and a total of six Frenchmen in the top ten. Ironically, stage two was won by the amateur Max Bulla of Austria – the first of the so-called *touristes-routiers* to wear the yellow jersey.

NICKNAMES OF TOUR RIDERS

Jacques Anquetil: *Maître Jacques*
Hippolyte Aucouturier: *Le Terrible*
Federico Bahamontés: *The Eagle of Toledo*
Gino Bartali: *Il Pio* (The Pious)
Ottavio Bottecchia: *The Bricklayer of Friuli*
Claudio Chiappucci: *El Diablo* (The Devil)
Mario Cipollini: *Super-Mario; The Lion King*
Fausto Coppi: *Il Campionissimo* (The Champion of Champions); *The Heron*
Roger de Vlaeminck: *The Gypsy*
Laurent Fignon: *The Professor*
Maurice Garin: *The Little Chimney Sweep*
Charly Gaul: *The Angel of the Mountains*
Walter Godefroot: *The Bulldog of Flanders*
Bernard Hinault: *The Badger*
Miguel Indurain: *Big Mig*
Octave Lapize: *La Frisé* (The Curly-Haired)
Antonin Magne: *The Taciturn*
Eddy Merckx: *The Cannibal*
Johan Museeuw: *The Lion of Flanders*
Marco Pantani: *Il Pirata* (The Pirate); *Elefantino*
Lucien Pothier: *The Butcher of Sens*
Raymond Poulidor: *Pou-Pou*
Tony Rominger: *The Hammer*
Tom Simpson: *Four-stone Coppi*
Jan Ullrich: *The Kaiser*

TOUR TRIVIA

Benoît Faure of France was renowned as a brilliant climber, but an atrocious descender. In 1930 he proved the point by losing more time coming down the Aubisque, Tourmalet and Soulor than he had made by going up them.

☆ TOUR STARS BORN IN 1930

Brian Robinson: The first British rider to finish the Tour when he came 29th in 1955, and the first to win a stage that he managed three years later. Yorkshire-born Robinson competed in seven Tours between 1955 and 1961, abandoning only two of them. His highest placing was fouteenth in 1956.

1931: BRAVO MAGNE

The whole of France was desperate for a French winner of the Tour, so there was understandable rejoicing when, in 1931, Antonin Magne rode into the Parc des Princes in the yellow jersey of race leader. It had been yet another murderous Tour, but Magne – who had trained by competing in the Giro d'Italia and by setting up a training camp in the Pyrenees – was a worthy winner. However, he was also very aware of the weight of responsibility of being the great white hope of France.

'If I had to suffer the mental anguish of the last month again, I wouldn't start it again for all the money in the world,' he said. 'The fatigue is nothing, the pain isn't much worse, but the fear of winning was truly horrible to me.'

TOUR TRIVIA

Riders in the Tour de France expend 5,000 calories on a flat stage, and over 8,000 a day in the mountains. The daily calorie expenditure of a typical man is around 2,500.

1932: LEDUCQ CASHES IN

André Leducq was the heart-throb of France, who regularly had to battle his way through crowds of female admirers waiting to greet him at the end of a stage. Leducq himself was very much aware of his own magnetism, and lent his name to all manner of consumer goods as a way of boosting his income. It's said that in the foothills of the Col de Bayard, he even took a few swigs from a bottle of white wine in order to ensure the vineyard sponsoring him got maximum publicity.

☆ TOUR STARS BORN IN 1932

Jan Adriaenssens: The teak-hard Belgian all-rounder who appeared in seven Tours between 1953 and 1961, coming third and wearing the yellow jersey on two occasions.

1933: DOUBLE DELIGHT FOR SPEICHER

Winner of the 1933 Tour was Frenchman Georges Speicher. Later that same year, the French selectors caused a storm when they refused to select Speicher for the World Championships. When one of the team riders dropped out on the eve of the race, a huge manhunt was ordered and Speicher was eventually found with his feet up in the local cinema. Despite not having trained for two months since the Tour, Speicher went on to win by five minutes, therefore becoming the first rider to complete the Tour–World Championship double.

TOUR TRIVIA

A police escort for the entire length of the Tour was introduced for the first time in 1933.

TOUR TRIVIA

Gears were allowed by the early Tour authorities, but there were only two. Changing gear involved stopping, removing the rear wheel, reversing it, and fixing it to the frame again.

TOUR TRIVIA

Spaniard Vincente Trueba became the first winner of the King of the Mountains competition at the 1933 Tour.

☆ TOUR STARS BORN IN 1933

Henry Anglade: A largely unpopular French rider, nicknamed Napoleon because he was short and bossy. He competed in ten Tours between 1957 and 1967, coming second in 1959.

1934: VIETTO GIVES HIS ALL

The great Antonin Magne had been winning stages of the Tour de France since 1927, and in 1931 clinched the race itself. So he was already a Tour legend when, in 1934, he set off in pursuit of yet another victory. Nicknamed 'The Taciturn', he must have cut a fearsome figure among younger riders in the peloton – none more so than René Vietto, an unknown 20-year-old drafted into the French team to the disbelief of many observers. But although Magne would indeed sweep to victory in Paris, it was the selfless exploits of Vietto that clinched the win and won the hearts of all Tour spectators.

The drama began in the Pyrenees, on the treacherous stage fifteen descent from l'Hospitalet to Ax-les-Thermes. Magne, wearing yellow since stage three, suddenly swerved and hit the deck, his front wheel smashed. Vietto, until then a peripheral figure in the team, obediently pulled over and handed over his bike. As Magne raced off down the mountain, Vietto sat on the safety wall and waited five minutes for the repair truck to arrive.

The next day, Vietto was with the leading bunch up the Col de Portet d'Aspet when he heard Magne shouting at him from behind. Yet again, the Tour leader had smashed his front wheel. There was nothing for it: Vietto turned and freewheeled down the mountain to give Magne his bike. This time as he sat and waited for assistance by the roadside, the tears flowed.

Although Vietto eventually finished fifth, he always maintained if it hadn't been for Magne's mechanical misfortune he would have won the Tour that year. He later described it as a 'hold-up'!

He was, perhaps, entitled to be bitter. During a thirteen-year career interrupted by six years of war, he wore the yellow jersey for a total of

26 days – and no rider has ever held it longer without actually winning the Tour itself.

TOUR TRIVIA

The crowds along the Champs Élysées that greeted Antonin Magne's 1934 Tour win were larger than those which celebrated the Armistice in 1918.

'The Tour today is nothing like what we rode or even the Tours of the after-war years. Equipment is better, the roads – above all those in the mountains – are nothing like the quagmires we sometimes had to ride through for hundreds of kilometres. It's not the same job. These days the Tour is a succession of little races.'

Louis Trousselier, winner of the 1905 Tour.

☆ TOUR STARS BORN IN 1934

Jacques Anquetil: One of the greats of cycling, Anquetil became the first man to win five Tours.

1935: DEATH IN THE RAVINE

Considering the horrendous road conditions and the unreliable bikes, it is something of a miracle that the first Tour fatality did not occur until 1935 – the 32nd running of the race. It happened on the Galibier, when Spaniard Francesco Cepeda misjudged a hairpin bend and plunged into a ravine, fracturing his skull. By the time the Tour doctor reached him several minutes later, Cepeda was already dead.

RIDERS WHO HAVE LED THE TOUR FROM START TO FINISH

- Maurice Garin (1903)
- Philippe Thys (1914)
- Ottavio Bottecchia (1924)
- Nicolas Frantz (1928)
- Romain Maes (1935)

1935: TRAINING RUN

Sometimes a moment of cycling inspiration can be enough to win the Tour de France. Sometimes you have to rely on a piece of outrageous good fortune. On the first stage of the 1935 Tour between Paris and Lille, the little-known Belgian Romain Maes had managed to break away from the peloton. The pack weren't unduly bothered: there were more than enough kilometres left to sweep him up. At the village of Haubourdin, however, Maes shot over a level crossing just seconds before the barriers came down. As the peloton waited furiously for the train to pass, Maes was pedalling hell-for-leather for the finish line. He won the stage by two minutes – and would not relinquish the yellow jersey again.

1935: BOOZE BREAK

Struggling along in stifling heat on the stage from Pau to Bordeaux, the riders thought they were seeing a mirage when up ahead they spotted a line of trestle tables laden with ice cold beer. It was no illusion, and pretty soon the entire peloton had stopped by the roadside to quench their thirst. All, that is, except Julien Moineau, an unknown French rider, who immediately put his head down and sped away to win the stage by several minutes. It later transpired that Moineau had organised the impromptu beer break with his pals, trusting that it would delay the peloton sufficiently for him to make his decisive break.

☆ TOUR STARS WHO DIED IN 1935

Henri Pélissier, aged 46: He was the eldest of the three Pélissier brothers who competed in the Tour de France over a period of more than twenty years between 1912 and 1935. Although he only finished two of the eight Tours he appeared in, Henri was by far the most successful, coming second in 1914 and winning in 1923. He was never a favourite of Henri Desgrange, however, who often accused him of being lazy and arrogant. Indeed, Pélissier was a vain, self-obsessed man outside of sport, and this was to be his undoing: his first wife shot herself after being driven to despair by him, and his 26-year-old girlfriend shot him five times after a row in which he had slashed her face with a kitchen knife. She was later given a year's suspended sentence after pleading self-defence.

1936: GODDET TAKES OVER

Although he was not a rider, Jacques Goddet had an ideal pedigree to take over as Tour organiser from Henri Desgrange. His father, Victor, was the accountant at *L'Auto* who gave Desgrange the money to launch the world's greatest cycle race in 1903. Goddet's first move upon being appointed was to allow gears to be used – something which Desgrange always rejected. In fact, compared to Desgrange, Goddet was a philanthropist when it came to the welfare of the riders. It was he who brought an end to the gruelling, all-day stages, although he always claimed that in order to keep the Tour special 'excess is necessary'. In the era of TV coverage, Goddet was more recognisable than some of the great riders of the 1960s and 1970s: he always travelled standing up through the sunroof of his red car, wearing jungle fatigues and a pith helmet. He was race organiser for 50 years, and for many people he *was* the Tour de France. On his death in 2000, French prime minister Lionel Jospin paid tribute when he said that Goddet had 'made the Tour de France, through his 50 years at the helm, the most popular French sports event and the one most known around the world.'

LANTERNE MEANS LAST

If you can't win the Tour, then the next best thing is to come last. At least that's the philosophy among the also-rans of the peloton for whom the position of *lanterne rouge* (red lamp) has become a highly sought-after means of publicity. Initially any rider who came in last overall after the second stage was kicked out of the race, but in the 1950s the idea of acknowledging riders who struggled manfully to complete the Tour without abandoning or finishing outside the time limit gained in popularity. During boring intermediate stages, the race to be last can often eclipse the battle for the *maillot jaune*, with riders in the frame for the *lanterne rouge* vying with each other to see who could go slowest without being expelled for exceeding the time limit. In 1968, Englishman John Clarey, who would finish nearly three hours behind winner Jan Janssen, made a name for himself by pretending to spray his moustache with rose fertiliser each morning 'for added strength'.

1936: FIRST AFRICAN RIDER

With war clouds once again gathering over Europe, in 1936 there were no Italian riders in the Tour. Instead, the numbers were made up by riders from Yugoslavia, Romania, Holland and Switzerland, and by 30 amateurs including the Algerian Abd-el-Kader Abbès, who became the Tour's first African rider.

TOUR TRIVIA
Until 1935, when aluminium came into use, wheel rims were made out of light wood.

TOUR TRIVIA
The Belgian rider Félicien Vervaecke was hit with a ten-minute penalty after he was discovered using a bike fitted with derailleurs (an automatic gear-changing mechanism) while climbing the Aubisque in 1936.

TOUR TRIVIA
Record numbers of spectators watched the 1936 Tour, thanks largely to the recently elected French Popular Front, who had promised the voters paid public holidays.

ANATOMY OF A LEGEND: GINO BARTALI

1937 saw the return of the Italians, and the Tour debut of one of the greatest riders of all time: the 23-year-old Gino Bartali. A craggy-faced and unassuming country boy from Tuscany, Bartali was nicknamed *Il Pio*, The Pious, because of his strong Catholic convictions and his overriding belief that whenever he raced, God was on his side – although his pioneering use of Campagnolo gears may have more directly helped him up the mountains.

Bartali was born in Ponte-a-Ema near Florence in 1914, where he died in 2000 aged 86. In 1936, Bartali had to be persuaded to continue racing after his brother Giulio was killed in a bike crash. Such was *Il Pio's* subsequent dominance, his opponents must have rued that particular decision. By the time he arrived at the Tour, he had already won the Giro d'Italia in 1936 and 1937.

Although he would crash out of his debut Tour, his stage victory in Grenoble earned him the yellow jersey and served notice of what was to come. Sure enough, the following year Bartali crushed the opposition, grabbing the King of the Mountains jersey on his way to Tour victory.

Legend has it that when he arrived at the end of a stage in Aix-les-Bains, a policeman held back the crowds with the words, 'Don't touch! He's a God!' During the war, Bartali helped thousands of Jews to escape deportation – an act which made him even more of a national hero afterwards.

Bartali's ding-dong rivalry with fellow countryman Fausto Coppi, particularly in the Giro, ignited the sport and divided a nation in the immediate post-war years. The contrast between the devout country boy and the urbane city-slicker was in many ways a precursor of the battle between the French riders Raymond Poulidor and Jacques Anquetil in the 1960s. The difference was that Bartali was nearly a decade older than Coppi, and was seen as a fading force compared to the young buck from

Milan. With this in mind, his astonishing Tour victory in 1948 – at the age of 34 and ten years after his last win – was seen by many as a final riposte to the young pretender.

In 1949 Coppi won the Tour, and although Bartali won a stage, it would be the last time he would wear yellow. He competed in four more Tours, finishing a creditable eleventh in his last at the age of 39.

▲▲ LEGENDARY MOUNTAINS OF THE TOUR: COL DE LA RÉPUBLIQUE

One of the few mountains to have been included in the Tour from its very first year, the République is one of the stand-out climbs of the Massif Central area. At 3,809 ft (1,161 m) it is by no means the highest mountain, nor the steepest – but it has been steeped in history ever since Hippolyte Aucouturier became the first rider to cross its summit in 1903. The following year, *L'Auto's* Géo Lefèvre was forced to fire his gun into the air to disperse a crowd of thugs who were threatening to beat up one of the riders on the climb (see Cheating and Skulduggery, page 12). At the summit of the mountain is a memorial to Paul de Vivrie, a well-known cycling journalist who was one of the early proponents of derailleur gears.

1937: HOLLAND – THE PRIDE OF BRITAIN

The 1937 Tour saw the first appearance of British riders. Bill Burl and Charlie Holland were part of an Anglo-Canadian team which were largely there to make up the numbers. They competed gamely but ultimately hopelessly; indeed, only Holland made it beyond the second stage. His Tour ended on stage fifteen, when he reached the finish line in

Luchon so late that the entire Tour entourage had already packed up and left. It would be another eighteen years before the Brits would make another appearance in the Tour.

1937: WHEN PUSH COMES TO SHOVE

Roger Lapébie broke the monopoly of Belgian Tour wins in 1937, but his victory was overshadowed with rumours of cheating and conspiracy. Specifically, it was alleged that Lapébie's untypical brilliance in the mountains was due to the fact that he had not only been pushed by French spectators on the roadside, but that he had grabbed hold of team and press cars in order to get a pull. When Henri Desgrange decided to penalise Lapébie a paltry 90 seconds, the outraged Belgian riders complained. At this, the French team threatened to go on strike if the penalty was increased. Lapébie eventually won the Tour by seven minutes, but the feeling of mutual antipathy between the Belgians and the French continued to rumble on afterwards. In an attempt to appease the Belgians, Desgrange announced that Lapébie would not be invited back to defend his title in 1938. The Belgians, understandably, were left wondering why this punitive action hadn't been taken during the race.

TOUR TRIVIA

1938 was the first year that derailleur gears were allowed in the Tour. These enabled the rider to shift gears with a lever, rather than having to stop, get off the bike and turn the wheel around.

Vive Le Tour

☆ TOUR STARS BORN IN 1937

Vittorio Adorni: An Italian rider briefly seen as the man to succeed Fausto Coppi and Gino Bartali, but who never lived up to his potential. He appeared in three tours, finishing only one in tenth position in 1964.

Rudi Altig: A fearsomely competitive German who surely would have enjoyed greater success than just one Points win in 1962 had his career not coincided with that of Jacques Anquetil.

Tom Simpson: The finest English-born cyclist ever to ride the Tour, he would become a huge celebrity both at home and abroad before dying tragically on Mont Ventoux in 1967.

1938: THE END OF THE ROAD FOR TWO GREATS

The 1938 Tour was to be the last for two great winners of the race. Antonin Magne and André Leducq – both 34 years old, born just twelve days apart, and both double winners of the Tour – celebrated the end of an era by engineering a two-man breakaway towards the end of the final stage into Paris. The two men entered the Parc des Princes together, and crossed the finish line hand-in-hand to the rapturous applause of 50,000 adoring French cycling fans.

1939: HIGH-SPEED CLIMBING

Stage sixteen of the 1939 Tour, 39 miles (64 km) between Bonneval-sûr-Arc and Bourg St Maurice, was the first-ever mountain time trial. It was won by Sylvère Maes of Belgium, the eventual winner of the race.

'Days pass and this group of men, powering along the roads of France, carry in their wake the enthusiastic camaraderie of the regions through which they pass. The Tour de France is an armistice called before the gathering storm.'

Henri Troyat, journalist, 1939

1939: AU'VOIR, HENRI

The 1939 Tour was the last before World War Two. It was also the last for Henri Desgrange. The Father of the Tour died on 16 August 1940 in Beauvallon, at the age of 75. A monument was erected to him on the summit of the Galibier, his favourite mountain, and the post of Tour *directeur*, which Desgrange had held for 36 years, was passed to his faithful lieutenant Jacques Goddet.

TOUR TRIVIA
Antonin Magne won 39 yellow jerseys during his long and successful career – but lost them all when the Germans invaded France in 1940.

☆ TOUR STARS WHO DIED IN 1939

Louis Trousselier, aged 57: One of the early Tour pioneers, Trousselier won on his debut in 1905 while on leave from the French army. In all, he competed in eight Tours until World War Two broke out in 1914, winning a total of thirteen stages. A born showman, Trousselier once set off on the descent of the Col de Porte with his feet on the handlebars.

TOUR WINNERS 1919–1939

1919: Fermin Lambot (BEL)

1920: Philippe Thys (BEL)

1921: Léon Scieur (BEL)

1922: Fermin Lambot (BEL)

1923: Henri Pélissier (FRA)

1924: Ottavio Bottecchia (ITA)

1925: Ottavio Bottecchia (ITA)

1926: Lucien Buysse (BEL)

1927: Nicolas Frantz (LUX)

1928: Nicolas Frantz (LUX)

1929: Maurice Dewaele (BEL)

1930: André Leducq (FRA)

1931: Antonin Magne (FRA)

1932: André Leducq (FRA)

1933: Georges Speicher (FRA) [KoM: Vicente Trueba (ITA)]

1934: Antonin Magne (FRA) [KoM: René Vietto (FRA)]

1935: Romain Maes (BEL) [KoM: Félicien Vervaecke (BEL))

1936: Sylvère Maes (BEL) [KoM: Julian Berrendero (SPA)]

1937: Roger Lapébie (FRA) [KoM: Félicien Vervaecke (BEL)]

1938: Gino Bartali (ITA) [KoM: Gino Bartali]

1939: Sylvère Maes (BEL) [KoM: Sylvère Maes]

FARM BOYS AND CITY
SLICKERS
1947–1960

L'END OF *L'AUTO*

One casualty of the war was *L'Auto*, the sports paper that had become synonymous with the Tour de France. It had turned to reporting war news, but five years without a Tour had proved disastrous to its circulation, and in August 1944 – amid allegations that it had been sympathetic to the Germans – the publication folded. Almost immediately a new sports paper started up. *L'Équipe* (The Team) was edited by former *L'Auto* journalist Jacques Goddet – who of course had taken over the running of the Tour from Desgrange in 1936.

A TOUR BY ANY OTHER NAME

The occupying Germans had no objection to the running of a Tour de France during the war, but rightly Jacques Goddet refused on the grounds that the event would inevitably be hijacked by the Nazis as a publicity opportunity. But although there was no Tour from 1940 to 1945, nor in 1946 as France once again set about rebuilding its shattered infrastructure, this is not to say there was no cycle racing. In 1942, the Circuit de France was held, which, although restricted to Frenchmen, was a full 941 miles (1,515 km) loop of the country and was won by François Neuville. In 1943 and 1944 this Grand Prix du Tour de France was won by Jo Goutourbe and Maurice de Simplaere, respectively. In 1946 two events were staged: the Ronde de France, and the Course du Tour de France. The latter, following the death of Henri Desgrange six years earlier, was sponsored and organised by *Le Parisien Libéré* and *L'Équipe*, and included such seasoned Tour riders as Jean Robic and René Vietto. As a dry run for the resumption of the Tour in 1947, it was a great success. Once again the public's appetite for *Le Vrai Tour* had been whetted.

1947: TRIALS AND TRIBULATIONS

The 1947 Tour featured the longest time trial in the event's history – a whopping 86 mile (139 km) slog from Vannes to St Brieuc. For the ageing René Vietto, it was a stage too far. Despite wearing yellow for fourteen of the race's eighteen stages, the seemingly cursed Vietto ran out of steam on the long time trial and slumped agonisingly back into fifth place. The Tour itself was won by Jean Robic, a rider who had emerged in those war-years races, and who snatched an improbable debut victory with a last-gasp break on the very last stage into Paris. He had won the world's greatest bike race without once wearing the yellow jersey.

1947: HATS OFF TO SWEETIE-PIE

Jean Robic had fractured his skull in a crash during the 1946 Paris–Roubaix classic and, as a result, was one of the few riders in the peloton to wear a protective leather helmet. This, rather unfairly, led to wolfwhistles and catcalls from his rivals, who gleefully nicknamed him *Briquet*, meaning 'Ducky' or 'Sweetie-pie'. Robic would reply, 'Bobet? Bartali? I've got one in each leg.' No, as ripostes go it was not up there with the best – but in 1947 'Briquet's' dramatic Tour win gave him deserved bragging rights among the peloton.

1947: TOE THE LINE

Apo Lazarides was a dedicated *domestique* who would do anything for his team leader René Vietto – and proved it in 1947, when Vietto ordered him to cut off his toe. Vietto himself was already down to nine toes after instructing the team doctor to snip one of them off in order to ease an aching foot. Lazarides dutifully agreed to the amputation, and for the rest of his life he would walk with a limp. Vietto's toe, incidentally, was pickled in formaldehyde and is kept in a bar in Marseilles.

TOUR TRIVIA
Pipped on the very last day of the 1947 Tour by Jean Robic, Pierre Brambilla is reputed to have buried his bike in his garden in disgust.

TOUR TRIVIA
The Italian rider Edouard Fachleitner, who finished second in the 1947 Tour, phoned home every evening to talk to his dog.

☆ TOUR STARS WHO DIED IN 1947

Jules Banino, aged 75: The oldest man to ride the Tour, at the age of 51 in 1924, Banino was a policeman who rode two Tours as an amateur, finishing neither. A corinthian of the finest sort, Banino abandoned in 1924 and elected to cycle home to Nice along the same road as the Tour would be taking a few hours later. In a classic misunderstanding, soon after setting off, the lead riders heard on the grapevine that a rider was ahead of them. After chasing him down they were horrified to learn that Banino was an amateur — so they beat him up and threw him in a ditch without waiting to hear how he had also disqualified himself from the race.

1948: BARTALI SAVES THE DAY

Gino Bartali won the Tour for Italy in 1948. But did he also save his country from anarchy? After twelve stages the ageing *Il Pio* was fully 21 minutes behind the leader Louison Bobet. During the rest day, however, events south of the Alps changed everything when a Sicilian hitman shot Palmiro Togliatti, chairman of the Communist Party, four times. As Togliatti fought for his life, Italy was paralysed by a general strike and across the country riots broke out.

Sometime that night Bartali received a telephone call from Alcide de Gaspari, leader of the rival Christian Democratic Party. His message was plain: the only way to stop Italy falling into civil war was for something — or someone — to distract the population.

The next day, Bartali the great patriot set out on a huge Alpine stage which took in the climbs of the Izoard, Lauteret, Galibier and Croix-de-Fer on the way to Aix-les-Bains. By the end of it, Bobet's lead had been shattered and Bartali led the Tour by over six minutes.

In Italy, the population listened on their radios and went wild with excitement. Two days later the Communists called off their strike as news of Bartali's win and Togliatti's recovery filtered through. Bartali went on to win the Tour, but his greatest victory that year was preventing the collapse of his homeland.

☆ TOUR STARS BORN IN 1948

Bernard Thévenet: A French rider who rode eleven Tours between 1970 and 1981, winning in 1975 and 1977. His lasting fame, however, is as the man who ended Eddy Merckx's reign by cracking him on the Col d'Allos in 1975.

ANATOMY OF A LEGEND: FAUSTO COPPI

In 1948 Gino Bartali crushed the field to win his second Tour de France at the age of 34. But if the Italian's victory left French cycling fans in despair, then worse was to come. The following year saw the arrival of Fausto Coppi.

Coppi was born in Tortona, northern Italy, on 15 February 1919. He first learned to cycle by running errands for a butcher. His first prize was a pound of sausages.

While Gino Bartali's humanitarian exploits during the war had made him a national hero, Coppi had been languishing in a POW camp after being captured by the British in Tunisia. As a prisoner of war, Fausto Coppi shared a plate with a fellow prisoner called Chiappucci; Chiappucci's son Claudio would become a hugely talented Tour rider.

His first race back in July 1945 was the Circuit of Aces in Milan. After four years without racing, he won at an average speed of 26 mph

(42 kph). In 1946 he sprang back into the limelight by winning the Milan–San Remo classic, and the following year he won the Giro d'Italia. Two years later, Coppi won the Giro again – but this time he planned to launch his assault on the Tour, thereby attempting to complete the Holy Grail of a Giro–Tour double.

Fausto Coppi's cycling career was remarkable, but it could never match his private life for drama. In 1953, he caused a sensation when he left his wife and shacked up with a married woman called Giulia Occhini. Such was the outrage in Italy that the local police broke into their hotel room to see if the two of them were sharing the same bed. The Pope was so outraged by Coppi's affair that he refused to give his traditional blessing to the Giro d'Italia unless he went back to his wife. Coppi applied for a divorce, but it was refused.

Despite his exploits, Coppi could never match the popularity of his fellow countryman Gino Bartali. Much of the opprobrium was a result of his affair and his frank views about drug-taking. When asked by one journalist if he took performance enhancing drugs, Coppi simply shrugged and said, 'Only when necessary.' When asked when it was necessary, he replied, 'Practically all the time.'

He died of malaria in 1960. His funeral was attended by 5,000 people including a paraplegic who claimed he had been able to walk since Coppi had given him 10,000 lire.

'He caresses rather than grips the handlebars; at the end of each pedal stroke his ankles flex gracefully; all the moving parts turn in oil. His long face appears like the blade of a knife as he climbs without apparent effort, like a great artist painting a watercolour.'

André Leducq describes the great Fausto Coppi

1949: THE OLD ONE-TWO

Coppi and Bartali were team-mates, but getting them to work together was never simple.

In 1949 Italian team manager Alfredo Binda persuaded the two men that by working together, Coppi and the now veteran Bartali could blow the race apart. So it proved – although initially Coppi took a great deal of convincing that Binda wasn't showing favouritism to Bartali, especially when, after a crash during a breakaway, Coppi discovered that the team's spare bike had already been handed to the older man who was way back at the rear of the field. As the race crossed the Alps, however, the two Italians finally got their act together in devastating fashion. A break on the Col d'Izoard gained them a lead of four minutes over the rest of the pack; by the end of the stage Bartali was in yellow, with Coppi just a minute behind.

The following day proved decisive as, once again, Coppi and Bartali shot away. With less than 31 miles (50 km) left, Bartali punctured. Coppi waited dutifully, but as *Il Pio* remounted he slipped and twisted his ankle. Word came from Binda that Coppi should ride on his own, and the man who would be dubbed 'The Heron' needed no second invitation to open his wings. At the end of that day, Coppi led Bartali by five minutes and the rest of the field by more than ten. The Tour was his, as was the elusive double.

PARIS BY ANY OTHER NAME

The Tour has always finished in Paris, although the now-famous sprint up and down the Champs Élysées was not introduced until 1975. Before then, the finishing line was found at:

1903–1905: Restaurant Père Auto on the outskirts of Paris (finishers then rode in procession to the track at Parc des Princes).

1906–1967: Parc des Princes.

1968–1975: Piste Municipale, Vicennes.

THE POINTS SYSTEM

Every year two separate battles are fought outside that for overall champion: the sprinters vie for the green jersey, the climbers for the polka-dot jersey of King of the Mountains. Each jersey is decided on points which are awarded at the end of sprints and mountain summits.

Green Jersey Points		
Flat Stage Finish	1st–2nd–3rd...25th	35–30–26...1
Mountain Stage Finish	1st–2nd–3rd...20th	25–22–20...1
High Mountain Stage Finish	1st–2nd–3rd...15th	20–17–15...1
Intermediate Sprint	1st–2nd–3rd	6–4–2
Individual Time Trial	1st–2nd–3rd...10th	15–12...1

Mountain Points (Polka-Dot Jersey)

Hors Catégory	1st–2nd–3rd...15th	40–35–30...1
Category 1	1st–2nd–3rd...12th	30–26–22...1
Category 2	1st–2nd–3rd...10th	20–15–12...1
Category 3	1st–2nd–3rd...5th	10–7–5...1
Category 3	1st–2nd–3rd	5 – 3 – 1

TOUR TRIVIA

The Tour was first broadcast on television in 1949. Cameras were set up in the Parc des Princes to record the arrival of stage winner Rik van Steenbergen and *maillot jaune* winner Fausto Coppi.

1950: STICKING IT TO THE LEGEND

He was a legend in Italy, but the great Gino Bartali could not always rely on the goodwill of cycling fans elsewhere. As the 1950 Tour passed through the Pyrenees, Bartali found himself being kicked and punched by overzealous French fans lining the route. On one occasion, he was actually knocked off his bike. Fed up with this treatment, Bartali led a revolt, which resulted in the withdrawal that night of the entire Italian team. But if the French thought the way was now clear for one of their men to win the race, they were to be sorely disappointed as Ferdi Kübler became the first Swiss rider to win the Tour.

TOUR TRIVIA

Ferdi Kübler was known as 'The Swiss Cowboy' on account of his fondness for wide-brimmed hats.

1950: AN UNEXPECTED DIP IN FORM

Racked with controversy after the withdrawal of Bartali and the Italian team, the 1950 Tour still found time to unwind. On the long stage between Toulon and Menton, the race swept past the glittering azure waters of the Gulf of St Tropez. Frazzled by the relentless 100 degree heat, the sight was too much for some of the riders, who pulled over and ran into the sea. Pretty soon around half of the peloton had joined in, splashing about with abandon. Tour director Jacques Goddet, following by car, didn't know whether to laugh or cry. 'Surely the cyclists should have been acquiring – or re-acquiring – the rudiments of their strenuous profession, instead of indulging in these carnival antics,' he said.

TOUR TRIVIA

Algerian Marcel Molines became the first – and so far only – black rider to win a stage of the Tour de France when he nipped in to win the stage between Perpignan and Nîmes in 1950.

1951: A BREAK TO REMEMBER

The Tour is littered with legendary breaks, when one rider suddenly gets clear of the peloton and, for dozens of lonely kilometres, fights a lonely battle to win the stage. Great escapes go hand in hand with great riders:

Bartali, Coppi, Charly Gaul, Eddy Merckx, Bernard Hinault and Miguel Indurain have all produced moments of glory etched in Tour history. But one of the greatest came in 1951 by a rider who was virtually unknown outside his native Switzerland but would win the Tour that year with five stages including an epic 86 mile (140 km) escape on the stage between Brive and Agen.

His name was Hugo Koblet, and when he got away from the pack after just 18 miles (30 km), nobody raised an eyebrow. It was one of those classic moments when the peloton's collective superiority is undermined by the determination of a solo rider – but mostly by its own lumbering inability to react to danger before it is too late. By the time Koblet was 43 miles (70 km) from the finish line, he was already five minutes ahead of the pack who were still stuck in the mountains. By the time he crossed the line, he had won the stage by more than two and a half minutes after a gruelling four hours of solo riding, and was observed idly combing his hair as he waited for the rest of the field to arrive.

'In the ten years I've raced I have never seen such a feat,' said Fiorenzo Magni. 'If there were two Koblets in the sport,' said Raphael Geminiani, 'I would retire from cycling tomorrow.'

Despite their magnanimous words, few of the riders expected Koblet to survive to Paris after such a lung-bursting effort. And he certainly wasn't a threat for the overall classification, being a full eight minutes behind the leader Wim van Est. But Koblet proved them all wrong. When van Est – the first Dutchman to wear yellow – crashed out on the Aubisque, the race was suddenly wide open. The next day, Koblet produced a blistering ride over the Tourmalet before outgunning the great Fausto Coppi in a sprint for yellow. He would not lose the jersey again, and was crowned Tour champion after one of the most amazing performances in the history of the event.

1951: WRONG TURN FOR WIM

Dutchman Wim van Est was leading the 1951 Tour and determined to remain in yellow as he began a helter-skelter descent of the Col d'Aubisque. The mountain has a deserved reputation as one of the most dangerous of the Tour, and on that day van Est proved why. Having already lost control on one tight hairpin, he continued on his way for a couple of hundred yards before slewing out of control and over the edge of the ravine. Fortunately, he was able to scramble back up and onto his bike. Anyone else perhaps would have thought twice about descending so recklessly – but not van Est. And it wasn't long before the Dutchman lost control again. This time both he and his bike plunged 100 feet into the ravine, and to everyone watching it was clear he wouldn't be getting up from this one. Miraculously, van Est was still alive. Even more remarkably, he was able to climb back out of the ravine using a rope made of inner tubes from the Dutch support vehicle. To everyone's relief, the damaged state of van Est's bike and the fact that the supply of inner tubes was now ruined meant he was forced to continue his journey to the bottom of the mountain in the back of an ambulance.

Wim van Est, descending the Aubisque, misreads a bend

Crashing over the edge, landing 100ft down in a ravine

His team-mates tie their spare inner tubes together to make a rope

van Est is pulled to safety

1951: A NEW STARTING POINT

In 1951 the Tour began in Metz, the first time since 1926 that the race had started outside Paris. Staging the *Grand Départ* in a different city was to be an annual occurrence from now on, a forerunner of the Tour Prologues which often take the event out of France for the first few stages.

1952: AN ICONIC CLIMB

The 1952 Tour was the first to include the iconic climb of Alpe d'Huez. The mountain climbs over 3,280 ft (1,000 m) in just 8 miles (14 km) with the help of 21 switchback bends. At the top the road terminates at a ski centre, which makes it perfect as a stage finish. On several occasions, the climb has been used as a mountain time trial. The first Tour rider to reach the summit was Fausto Coppi, and his name is one of the many stage winners now immortalised on signs positioned at each bend. The record time for the ascent of the Alpe is still held by the late Marco Pantani, who blasted to the top in 37 minutes 35 seconds in 1997.

STAGE WINNERS IMMORTALISED ON ALPE D'HUEZ HAIRPINS

Bend Number	Riders Immortalised	Year of stage win
21	Fausto Coppi, Lance Armstrong	1952, 2001
20	Joop Zoetemelk, Iban Mayo	1976, 2003
19	Hennie Kuiper, Lance Armstrong	1977, 2004
18	Hennie Kuiper	1978
17	Joachim Agostinho	1979
16	Joop Zoetemelk	1979*
15	Peter Winnen	1981
14	Beat Breu	1982
13	Peter Winnen	1983
12	Luis Herrera	1984
11	Bernard Hinault	1986
10	Federico Echave	1987
9	Steven Rooks	1988
8	Gert-Jan Theunisse	1989
7	Gianni Bugno	1990
6	Gianni Bugno	1991
5	Andy Hampsten	1992
4	Roberto Conti	1994
3	Marco Pantani	1995
2	Marco Pantani	1997
1	Giuseppe Guerini	1999

TOUR TRIVIA

In 1952 the ski centre at the top of Alpe d'Huez consisted of just three small hotels. The road was pot-holed and there seemed to be very little to entice the Tour there. That is until one of the hotel owners, Georges Rajon, got together with two other businessmen to offer an incentive of

2,000 francs to the Tour organisers to bring the peloton to the 21 hairpins. The Tour did not return there until 1976 – when Monsieur Rajon once again forked out for the privilege of having the world's best riders racing to his hotel.

1952: COMBAT CHAMP

The combativity award is presented at the end of every day to the rider who, in the opinion of a panel of experts, has produced the most competitive ride, whether in a solo break or on a mountain stage. It was introduced in 1952, and the daily prize was 100 francs. Since 1998 the winner of the previous day's award is identified by a red number on his back rather than the usual white one..

1952: BROTHERS IN ARMS

Fausto Coppi returned to the Tour in 1952 just a year after a devastating personal tragedy made him question his own career. His younger brother Serse, a talented rider in his own right, hit his head in a fall during a sprint in the Giro del Piedmonte. After returning to his hotel, the young Italian suffered a brain haemorrhage and died. Coppi was devastated, but found solace and encouragement in the unlikely form of his old rival Gino Bartali, whose own brother had been killed while racing in 1936. Like Bartali, Coppi was persuaded back onto the bike – and, like Bartali, he won the Tour.

'Never was it possible for us to write "Today Fausto was mistaken". His legs never betrayed him and neither did his brains. I ask myself if ever in the course of the history of the Tour de France a winner knew how to ally more strength to more wisdom, patience and intelligence. Irresistible as he had been in Paris–Roubaix, the lamb was transformed into a lion.'

André Leducq waxes lyrical again
about 1952 Tour winner Fausto Coppi

1952: BARTALI PASSES THE BATON

The relationship between Coppi and Bartali had always been frosty – but then, until 1952 both men had legitimately regarded themselves as Tour contenders. This year, however, there was simply no stopping Coppi. His performances in the mountains, and particularly the new climbs to the ski stations at Alpe d'Huez and Sestriere, were compared to a 'ski-lift gliding up its steel cable' by the awe-struck Jacques Goddet, and convinced Bartali – then 38 years old – that he could no longer compete with the younger man. In a symbolic moment, when Coppi punctured three times in just 12.5 miles (20 km) on the stage between Sestriere and Monaco, Bartali stopped and offered his great rival his wheel. Coppi took it, and in doing so accepted the baton of the great Italian cycle champions.

☆ TOUR STARS WHO DIED IN 1952

Maurice Dewaele, aged 56: The Belgian Dewaele rode in four Tours between 1927 and 1931, finishing third, second, fifth, and winning the event in 1929. His win was not universally popular, especially with Henri Desgrange who reckoned Dewaele had only won because long-time leader Victor Fontan suffered a series of mechanical mishaps in the Alps, culminating in falling into a ravine. In fact, Dewaele spent the last few days of the race in a state of exhaustion, being protected by his team-mates all the way into Paris. On witnessing his arrival as race winner, Desgrange grumbled, 'My race has been won by a corpse!'

1953: THE BOBET YEARS BEGIN

Having won a gruelling Giro in 1953, Fausto Coppi decided not to contest that year's Tour de France. Little did he know it, but at 34 years old, he would never wear yellow again. Instead, the 50th anniversary Tour was won, fittingly, by a Frenchman, Louison Bobet. Indeed, Bobet would become the first rider to achieve three victories in a row. In doing so, he began a tradition of one rider dominating the Tour that would be upheld in years to come by the likes of Anquetil, Merckx, Hinault, Indurain and Armstrong.

1953: BARTALI BOWS OUT

The 1953 Tour marked the end of Gino Bartali's career. The great Italian, now 39 years old, finished in eleventh place, a full 32 minutes behind the winner Louison Bobet.

1954: BOBET PEDIGREE

Although he had competed in five Tours, Louison Bobet was better known as a one-day rider. It has been argued, somewhat unfairly, that his win in 1953 owed more to the absence of Coppi and the strength of his

French team than his own cycling genius. Sure enough, Bobet came along as some of the great names of the previous era were winding down their careers – and in 1954, his second win was made easier by the absence of the entire Italian team due to a strike. But nevertheless, he was a courageous climber in the high mountains and a mean time-triallist, and winning three consecutive Tours in any era is an achievement that puts him up with the greats.

1954: THE TOUR GOES DUTCH

An estimated 100,000 spectators turned out in Amsterdam as the 1954 Tour was launched from a country other than France for the first time in its history. The 134 mile (216 km) stage to Braaschaat in Belgium was, fittingly, won by a Dutchman, Wout Wagtmans.

'He's a very good climber. But he's completely mad.'

Jesús Loroño, team-mate of the legendary Eagle of Toledo Federico Bahamontés, who made his Tour debut in 1954

THE COWARDY CUSTARD OF TOLEDO

As a climber, Federico Bahamontés – the Eagle of Toledo – was unrivalled. As a descender of the steep mountain passes, he was a disaster. It was not unknown for him to unclip his feet from his pedals and use them to skid round hairpin corners for fear of crashing.

In his first Tour, Bahamontés reached the top of the Galibier several minutes ahead of the rest of the peloton – but rather than risk an accident on a helter-skelter solo descent, he climbed off his bike, sat on a wall, and enjoyed an ice cream in the sunshine while he waited for the others to catch up. Officially, it was claimed his bike had developed a mechanical fault, but Bahamontés never denied it was because he was scared of the perilous descent. It would not be the last time his phobia would strike. In 1956 he threw his bike into a ravine rather than descend the Col de Luitel. One reason put forward to explain his phobia of descending is that during a race in Spain he crashed on a hairpin bend and landed against a cactus.

'I always did my best on really hot days because then my opponents couldn't take as much dope as they would have liked.'

Federico Bahamontés

☆ TOUR STARS BORN IN 1954

Bernard Hinault: The man known as 'The Badger' dominated the Tour in the late 1970s and early 1980s, becoming only the third rider in history to win five Tours.

1955: TV CATCHES UP WITH THE TOUR

Back in 1903 the pages of *L'Auto* were the only way of finding out what was happening in the Tour de France. Newspapers were gradually superseded by radio, and in 1955 the Tour was for the first time given television coverage. Although live transmission was many years away, cycling fans across France – at least those with access to a TV – could watch highlights from that day's stage just a few hours after the riders had crossed the finish line.

LEGENDARY MOUNTAINS OF THE TOUR: MONT VENTOUX

Mont Ventoux, the bleak, windswept giant of Provence, is a mountain that was first introduced to the Tour in 1951. It has become an inextricable part of the race's legend ever since. It was here, on its boulder-strewn summit, that Britain's Tom Simpson died in 1967, undone by dehydration and drugs – but fully twelve years earlier the Ventoux gave early warning of what it could do to even the toughest of riders. As the 1955 Tour made its way over the mountain in broiling heat, Jean Mallejac, who had worn the yellow jersey and eventually finished second in 1953, was clearly in difficulty. 'Streaming with sweat, haggard and comatose, he was zig-zagging and the road wasn't wide enough for him,' wrote journalist Jacques Augendre. 'He'd passed the stage where every pedal seemed to weigh 100 kg. He couldn't feel his legs or arms. Colours and shapes dissolved in front of him. He was already no longer in the real world, still less in the world of cyclists and the Tour de France.'

Mallejac eventually collapsed 6 miles (10 km) from the summit, his legs still turning phantom pedals. In the ambulance he had a fit, and there were grave fears for his life. It later transpired that the rider was up to his eyeballs with drugs.

While that drama was going on, further up the mountain the 1950 Tour winner Ferdi Kübler was having problems of his own. A violently aggressive rider, Kübler had been warned several times by his manager to go easy on the Ventoux, but to no avail. 'Ferdi is not like other riders!' he insisted.

Delirious and foaming at the mouth, Kübler was eventually forced to stop at a roadside café where he announced, 'Stand clear! Ferdi about to explode!' He then promptly jumped back on his bike and set off in the wrong direction, before a couple of drinkers turned him round. That evening at the finish in Avignon, Kübler announced his retirement.

'Ferdi killed himself on Ventoux,' he said. Sadly, he would not be the last.

BROTHERS ON THE BIKE

Cycling must be in the blood, judging by the large number of brothers who have competed in the Tour. They include:

- Maurice and César Garin
- Henri, Francis and Charles Pélissier
- Antonin and Pierre Magnin
- Roger and Guy Lapébie
- Louison and Jean Bobet
- Roger and Erik De Vlaeminck
- Jo and Eddy Plankaert
- Pascal, Régis, Jérôme and François Simon
- Marc and Yvone Madiot
- Stephen and Laurence Roche
- Miguel and Prudencio Indurain
- Laurent and Nicolas Jalabert

THE TALE OF THE GREEN JERSEY

Victories

6: Erik Zabel (1996, 97, 98, 99, 2000, 2001)
4: Sean Kelly
3: Jan Janssen, Eddy Merckx, Freddy Maertens,
    Djamolidine Abdoujaparov

Victories by nation

18: Belgium
9: France
8: Germany
4: Ireland, Netherlands
3: Uzbekistan, Australia
2: Switzerland
1: Italy

1955: SORE WINNER

Louison Bobet won his third successive Tour in 1955, although agonising
saddle sores picked up in the Pyrenees meant he had to ride most of the
last three stages standing out of his saddle.

'I salute him [Bobet] because he is a great champion, but I think if the
war had never taken place I too could have won three consecutive
Tours.'

Philippe Thys, three-time Tour winner (1913, 1914 and 1920), hails
Louison Bobet's third back-to-back victory in 1955

☆ TOUR STARS WHO DIED IN 1955

Maurice Archambaud, aged 49: Despite a love of food that was reflected
in his pot belly, Archambaud of France was a leading star in the 1930s.
He set the world hour record in 1937 with a distance of 28.48 miles
(45.84 km), and won Paris–Nice twice. In the Tour, he competed five
times between 1932 and 1936, wearing the yellow jersey once and
finishing no higher than fifth.

1956: ROGER THE DODGER

To win the Tour de France is a monumental achievement in any
circumstances, which is why you have to feel sorry for Roger Walkowiak
of France, who triumphed in 1956. Surely in the history of the race
there cannot have been a winner so universally dismissed as unworthy of
the title.

Okay, he did it without winning a stage – but he was hardly the first
to manage that. And it was hardly Walkowiak's fault that favourites such
as Luxembourg's Charly Gaul, Stan Ockers of Belgium, and Federico
Bahamontés of Spain were far too busy battling for the King of the
Mountains jersey to bother with the general classification.

Walkowiak was unfortunate because the 1956 Tour had been shorn of
the great heroes of cycling with the withdrawals of three-times winner
Louison Bobet and ageing former champions Coppi, Kübler and Koblet.
With the exception of Bobet, it's unlikely that any of them would have

been in the frame for Tour victory, but this did not stop the critics blaming Walkowiak for winning the Tour that nobody else seemingly wanted to win.

TOUR TRIVIA

If you want to be a Tour winner, be 29 years old. That's historically the most common age, with thirteen winners. Only 21 winners have been older than 30.

☆ TOUR STARS BORN IN 1956

Sean Kelly: Kelly was one of a rich crop of Irish riders who appeared on the European scene in the mid-1980s, which included Tour winner Stephen Roche. Hard as nails, the man from Waterford competed in fourteen Tours between 1978 and 1992, finishing all but two of them and winning the green 'points' jersey four times. In 1988, at the peak of his powers, he won the Vuelta in Spain. His greatest successes, however, came in the Paris–Nice race, which he won a staggering seven times, and in gruelling one-day Classics like Paris–Roubaix, Liège–Bastogne–Liège, and Milan–San Remo, where the distance, conditions and relatively flat terrain perfectly suited his attritional style. A taciturn man, Kelly was dubbed 'the only man who ever nodded in answer to a question on the radio'.

1957: THE ARRIVAL OF ANQUETIL

1957 saw the arrival on the scene of a rider who would dominate the Tour de France for much of the next decade, a man whose five Tour victories would set the benchmark for cycling excellence. And the nature of Jacques Anquetil's debut left no one in any doubt that he was the future of the sport. To win the Tour on your first attempt is remarkable enough, but to win it by more than fourteen minutes is practically unheard of. But then, Jacques Anquetil was a most remarkable rider.

Born in Mont-St-Aignan, near Rouen, in January 1934, Anquetil was not particularly well off, but for some reason was always perceived as being so – a fact that would form the basis of his rivalry with southern farmboy Jacques Poulidor in the 1960s, which itself mirrored that of Fausto Coppi and Gino Bartali twenty years earlier.

From the age of eighteen, Anquetil was already showing promise. He was a member of the 1952 French Olympic team which won bronze in the time trial; indeed his startling time-trialling ability was one of the main reasons for his Tour successes. He was not only lightning fast, he had the shrewd, calculating brain to know precisely how much effort to expend on the course and when to expend it.

In the early 1950s, Anquetil made his name by beating the likes of Louison Bobet in the Grand Prix of Nations, an 88 mile (143 km) time trial near Paris – an event he would win six times in a row and nine times in total.

When he entered his first Tour as a 23-year-old in 1957, few thought a pure time-trialler – even one as good as Anquetil – would survive the rigours of the Alps and the Pyrenees. But they were wrong. Unstoppable on the flat early stages, it was in the mountains that Anquetil won the Tour, holding off the challenge of Belgium's Marcel Janssens before finally destroying him in the final time trial.

A star was born.

'He [Anquetil] was the world's most beautiful pedalling machine.'

Jean-Paul Ollivier, French TV commentator

GAUL BLADDER

Charly Gaul of Luxembourg was rightly known as one of the sport's greatest climbers. Unfortunately he was also known as Monsieur Pi-Pi after perfecting the art of urinating while still in the saddle.

☆ TOUR STARS WHO DIED IN 1957

Maurice Garin, aged 84: The first winner of the Tour de France in 1903.

1958: THE ANGEL OF THE MOUNTAINS

After his stunning success in 1957, Jacques Anquetil was the overwhelming favourite to win the Tour the following year. However, he was dogged by illness and pulled out after the first stage, a fact that led to the unlikely figure of climber Charly Gaul winning all the time trials. This, along with his victory by 31 seconds on Mont Ventoux and a final mountain stage win of over eight minutes, secured a first and only Tour victory for the so-called Angel of the Mountains.

TOUR TRIVIA

Three years after becoming the first Englishman to complete the Tour de

France, Yorkshire-born Brian Robinson became the first to win a stage when he was first in a bunch sprint into Brest.

A TRAGIC TRIO

It had been more than twenty years since Spain's Francesco Cepeda had become the Tour's first and only fatality in 1935. In 1957 and 1958, however, the event was marred by three deaths – ironically, none of them riders. In 1957 the respected route broadcaster Alex Virot and his motorcycle driver René Wagner were killed when they plunged into a ravine near Ax-les-Thermes. Virot had been responsible for the first live radio coverage of the Tour in 1933. The following year, André Darrigade was at the head of a line of riders circling the Parc des Princes at the end of the race when he smashed into Constant Wouters, a stadium official, who was standing too close to the edge of the track. While Darrigade escaped with just five stitches in a head wound, Wouters was seriously injured and died eleven days later in hospital.

☆ TOUR STARS BORN IN 1958

Phil Anderson: British-born but with an Australian passport, Anderson was the first Aussie to wear the yellow jersey in 1981.

Robert Millar: The finest climber Britain has ever produced, in 1984 Glasgow-born Millar became the only Briton to win the King of the Mountains jersey, while his fourth place was Britain's best placing. He is also one of the only vegetarians to win the polka-dot jersey.

TOUR TRIVIA

Henry Anglade of France, second in 1959, was never a popular rider. He was known as 'Napoleon' in the peloton because of his appearance and his bossy manner. When he retired, Anglade learned how to make stained glass windows. One of his creations can be found at the Notre Dame des Cyclistes, a small chapel in southern France which has become a museum of old bikes and jerseys belonging to the world's greatest cyclists.

COPPI SUCCUMBS

At the age of 41, Fausto Coppi's days as a Tour legend were long gone. Instead, he was funding his retirement by turning out in lucrative exhibition races around the world. At the back end of 1959 Coppi found himself in Upper Volta, Africa (now known as Burkina Faso), combining some bike riding with a good amount of game hunting. It was not until his return to Italy at Christmas that he suddenly fell seriously ill – and by the time his doctors realised that he had contracted malaria it was too late. On 2 January 1960, Coppi died. The cycling world was stunned; Italy was in mourning.

☆ TOUR STARS BORN IN 1959

Steve Bauer: Without doubt the best rider to come from Canada, Bauer rode eleven Tours between 1985 and 1995, with his finest performance a fourth place, a stage win, and four days in the yellow jersey in 1988.

Stephen Roche: One of a hugely talented group of Irish riders, which included Sean Kelly and Martin Earley, that took European cycling by storm in the 1980s. Roche competed in ten Tours between 1983 and 1993, but his *annus mirabilis* was in 1987 when he not only became the first Irishman to win the Tour but also bagged the Giro d'Italia and the World Championship.

☆ TOUR STARS WHO DIED IN 1959

Charles Pélissier, aged 56: The youngest of three brothers who competed in the Tour in the 1920s and 1930s, Charles Pélissier rode six times between 1929 and 1935. He was a fine rider in his own right, winning eight stages in 1930 and five in 1931 – this normally would have been enough to win the Tour itself, but Pélissier was unfortunate in that he coincided with the era of national teams. Therefore, his hard work was directed towards the overall success of team leaders Andre Leducq and Antonin Magne.

Francis Pélissier, aged 64: The middle Pélissier, Francis was the least successful Tour rider. He rode five Tours between 1919 and 1927, but finished only one, in 1923. He did, however, wear the yellow jersey on his final appearance after winning the opening stage between Paris and Dieppe.

1960: CRY ME A RIVIÈRE

The tragic cloud that appeared to be hanging over the Tour showed no sign of disappearing in 1960. While furiously descending the Col du Perjuret in pursuit of the *maillot jaune* and eventual Tour winner,

Gastone Nencini of Italy, Roger Rivière – along with Anquetil, the most talented French cyclists of their generation – plunged off the narrow road and 50 feet into a ravine. His back was broken, and although it would not stop him walking again, his brief but brilliant riding career was over. Initially Rivière blamed his brakes for the crash, but it wasn't long before rumours started to circulate that Rivière was so pumped full of the tranquilliser Palfium, he had been unable to pull on his brake levers. The drug had even been found in the back pocket of his jersey after he crashed. With his career and his reputation in ruins, Rivière eventually admitted that he had been taking drugs as a matter of course. His 1958 world hour record was, he confessed, completed after huge injections of amphetamine and solucamphor.

THE SAD TRUTH

Roger Rivière's admission of routine drug-taking merely reinforced an unspoken truth about the Tour. Fausto Coppi had openly admitted taking drugs on a regular basis and even Jacques Anquetil, when asked his views on the matter, merely shrugged his shoulders and said, 'You cannot ride the Tour on water.'

TOUR TRIVIA

Arne Jonsson of Denmark was forced to abandon the 1960 Tour before it even started after thieves stole his cycling shoes on the eve of the race.

1960: ADIEU, MONSIEUR LE PRÉSIDENT!

Sometimes you've got to take a stage win whenever you can. Such was the case for lowly *domestique* Pierre Beuffeuil, who in 1960 pleaded ignorance in order to cross the finish line first. His moment of glory came when the Tour passed through Colombey-les-Deux-Églises, country residence of President Charles de Gaulle. The great French hero was at home that day, and at his request the riders paused at the gates of his house in order to shake hands and say hello. All, that is, except Beuffeuil, who knew nothing of this meeting and assumed there had been some sort of crash which had held up the peloton at the roadside. Without stopping to check, he set off pell-mell for the finish in Troyes and won the stage comfortably.

THE ERA OF ANQUETIL

The 1960 Tour brought to an end a decade in which the event had re-established itself after the war years and unearthed stars like Coppi, Bahamontés, Gaul and Bobet. Bikes were getting better, roads were improving, and the insane stages of the Desgrange era had long gone. It should have heralded a golden age of cycling to come. Yet as the 1960s dawned, there was a sense of foreboding among many traditional cycling fans for precisely those reasons. The days of the crazy amateur mending his own broken forks were over: the race now relied on team tactics and calculation. Endurance was no longer measured in miles and exposure to the elements; it was a question of knowing how to manipulate the human body to perform to order. Drugs had always been a part of the Tour – but there was a big difference between a swig of brandy and systematic pill-popping and amphetamine injections.

It was no surprise that the 1960s became the era of Jacques Anquetil, because if any rider was created to dominate this new, cold-blooded time, it was the man from Rouen.

☆ TOUR STARS BORN IN 1960

Laurent Fignon: A French rider who competed in ten Tours between 1983 and 1993, winning the race on his debut and completing the double the following year. Despite this, the pony-tailed and bespectacled Fignon is perhaps better known for blowing a 50 second lead on the final time trial to lose the 1989 Tour by eight seconds to Greg Lemond.

Steven Rooks: A talented Dutch rider who competed in eleven Tours between 1983 and 1994, claiming the King of the Mountains title on the way to coming second in 1988.

Sean Yates: A rock-solid English pro who competed in twelve Tours between 1984 and 1995. His finest moment came in 1994 when he wore the yellow jersey for the first and only time. That same year, the Tour came to Britain and Yates was allowed to lead the peloton as it passed through his home town of Forest Row in Sussex.

☆ TOUR STARS WHO DIED IN 1960

Émile Georget, aged 78: He competed in the first Tour in 1903, and a further nine until 1914. The Frenchman holds a place in Tour legend for becoming the first rider to climb the Galibier in 1911.

OUR WINNERS 1947–1960

1947: Jean Robic (FRA) [KoM: Pierre Brambilla (ITA)]

1948: Gino Bartali (ITA) [KoM: Gino Bartali]

1949: Fausto Coppi (ITA) [KoM: Fausto Coppi]

1950: Ferdi Kübler (SWI) [KoM: Jean Robic (FRA)]

1951: Hugo Koblet (SWI) [KoM: Raphael Geminiani (ITA)]

1952: Fausto Coppi (ITA) [KoM: Fausto Coppi]

1953: Louison Bobet (FRA) [KoM: Jesús Loroño (SPA); Points: Fritz Schaer (SWI)]

1954: Louison Bobet (FRA) [KoM: Federico Bahamontés (SPA); Points: Ferdi Kübler (SWI)]

1955: Louison Bobet (FRA) [KoM: Charly Gaul (LUX); Points: Stan Ockers (BEL)]

1956: Roger Walkowiak (FRA) [KoM: Charly Gaul (LUX); Points: Stan Ockers (BEL)]

1957: Jacques Anquetil (FRA) [KoM: Gastone Nencini (ITA); Points: Jean Forestière (FRA)]

1958: Charly Gaul (LUX) [KoM: Federico Bahamontés (SPA); Points: Jean Graczyk (FRA)]

1959: Federico Bahamontés (SPA) [KoM: Federico Bahamontés; Points: Andre Darrigade (FRA)]

1960: Gastone Nencini (ITA) [KoM: Imerio Massignan (ITA); Points: Jean Graczyk (FRA)]

MAÎTRE JACQUES AND MISTER TOM 1961–1968

1961: ANQUETIL SHOWS HE MEANS BUSINESS

On the morning of Sunday 25 June, the Tour de France set off from Rouen. It was the first part of a two-stage *Grand Départ* which would travel 84 miles (136 km) to Versailles before an afternoon time trial of just 17 miles (28 km). Perhaps it was because since winning the Tour on his debut in 1957 he had failed to finish (1958), finished a disappointing third (1959), or failed to start (1960); perhaps it was because the Tour was starting in his home town; or perhaps it was because of a bet he'd made before the start of the race – but Jacques Anquetil showed a ruthless determination to dominate the race right from the start. And it was a dream start. On the road to Versailles, Anquetil found himself in a breakaway of fifteen riders more than five minutes ahead of his main rivals Charly Gaul, Joseph Plankaert and Imerio Massignan. At the end of the time trial, Anquetil was wearing the yellow jersey – and would keep it all the way to Paris to win his wager. In the end, Anquetil won the Tour by twelve minutes; psychologically, he had succeeded in crushing some of the finest cyclists in the world.

TOUR TRIVIA

The *flamme rouge* is the red triangle suspended above the road which marks the beginning of the last kilometre of a stage.

'Repulsive dwarves, impotent, submissive, satisfied in their mediocrity.'

Jacques Goddet, Tour director, lambasts the riders who failed to attack Anquetil in 1961

☆ TOUR STARS BORN IN 1961

Tony Rominger: Swiss-born Rominger won three Tours of Spain and set the world hour record on two occasions, but could never crack the Tour de France in seven attempts between 1988 and 1997. The nearest he came was second in 1993, when he claimed the King of the Mountains jersey.

Greg Lemond: The first American to win the Tour, Lemond would win it three times in all, despite a near-death experience when he was shot during a hunting trip. His 1989 battle with Laurent Fignon remains perhaps *the* greatest duel in Tour history (see Eight Seconds, page 178).

TOUR TRIVIA

Rudi Altig of Germany was not only a gifted rider, winning the green jersey in 1962, he was something of an acrobat as well. He would often entertain crowds before a race by standing on his head, and one night he left a restaurant on his hands.

1962: SIMPSON WEARS YELLOW

Stage twelve of the 1962 Tour from Pau to Saint-Gaudens was won by Robert Cazala of France. However, the yellow jersey went to a skinny, beaky-nosed rider from the coalfields of Nottinghamshire. Tom Simpson would keep the *maillot jaune* for just one day; but it was the first time an Englishman – indeed English *speaker* – had ever worn the most hallowed jersey in the sport.

1962: ANQUETIL AGAIN

If Jacques Goddet had hoped his savage broadside at the 'repulsive dwarves' of the peloton would inspire the riders to at least challenge Jacques Anquetil in 1962, he was to be sorely disappointed. Although the record shows that Maître Jacques wore yellow for only the last three stages of the race, the opposition – with the honourable exception of Raymond Poulidor – failed to inflict any damage on the reigning champion. Once Gastone Nencini abandoned with food poisoning in the Pyrenees, Anquetil knew that all he had to do was remain in contention until the final time trial. Sure enough, Anquetil hammered the field by three minutes, giving him an overall and unassailable lead of five minutes over his nearest rival Joseph Plankaert.

TOUR TRIVIA
When asked by an eager young boy the best way to prepare for the Tour, Anquetil replied, 'With a good woman and a bottle of champagne.'

IN MEMORIAM

The Tour de France believes in honouring its legends, which is why France is littered with memorials to the great riders. They include:

Jacques Anquetil: in Quincampoix, a suburb of Rouen, and another by the track at the Piste Municipale in Paris.

Tom Simpson: at the spot on Mont Ventoux where he died in 1967.

Fausto Coppi: on the Izoard, next to one in memory of Louison Bobet.

Charles, Francis and Henri Pélissier: at the Piste Municipale in Paris.

Eddy Merckx: the Mourenx Vélodrome, where he won in 1969, is named after him.

Raymond Poulidor: a street named after him in his home town of Sauvat-sur-Vige.

Henri Desgrange: on the slopes of the Galibier.

René Pottier: at the summit of the Ballon d'Alsace.

Eugène Christophe: in the village of Marie-de-Campan at the foot of the Tourmalet, where he fixed his broken forks at the local forge in 1913.

Octave Lapize: at the summit of the Tourmalet.

René Vietto: at the top of the Col de Braus outside Nice.

Luis Ocaña: on the Col de Mente.

Wim van Est: on the spot where he fell into a ravine on the decent of the Aubisque.

1962: EVERYONE LOVES RAYMOND

The 1962 Tour saw the debut of a rider who would arguably become as famous as Jacques Anquetil and without doubt more popular. During the years of Anquetil's domination, Raymond Poulidor was one of the few riders prepared to challenge him for the yellow jersey, and the French public loved him for it. The fact that Pou-Pou, as he was known, was destined never to win the Tour – appearing fourteen times and finishing second on three occasions – made them love him all the more.

In the 1950s the rivalry between Coppi and Bartali had divided Italy.

Now the question of whether you supported aloof Anquetil or honest farmboy Poulidor divided France. To a certain extent it still does. In the Limousin area of the Massif Central, where Poulidor was born, there was no debate. Former Tour winner Antonin Magne once remarked, 'I know of farms in the Limoges area where his picture hangs between Bernadette Soubirous (the 14-year-old girl who claimed to have seen a vision of the Virgin Mary at Lourdes) and the picture of the family's late grandfather.'

Poulidor's gallant but ultimately unsuccessful attempts to win the Tour earned him the nickname 'The Eternal Second' – although Joop Zoetemelk finished runner-up on six occasions.

'He [Poulidor] always comes second, usually behind me. And still they shout more for him than for me. If he loses, he doesn't have to find excuses. But if I come second or third, then I've failed. They call me a calculator, a strategist, even if a miscalculation has just made me lose.'

Jacques Anquetil wonders why the French fans always love
Pou-Pou more

1962: GIVE THE GUY A BREAK

As he completed a lap of honour in the Parc des Princes having won his third Tour in convincing style, Jacques Anquetil was booed and jeered by several hundred spectators, indicating the level of dissatisfaction with the apparent ease with which he had won the race. 'Free to do so they emphatically were,' wrote one commentator. 'We doubt neither their rights nor their good faith, while holding serious reservations about their good manners. We recognise their right to question the merits of the champion. We only ask, in return, that they grant us the right not to share their opinions.'

1963: MEDDLERS MASSACRED

It was all very well criticising the peloton, but when Anquetil cruised to his third Tour win in 1962, the race organisers realised that something a little more tangible than caustic words was required. They duly reduced the distance of the individual time trials and placed the finish line of the mountain stages at the top of the final climb. The idea was to neutralise Anquetil's phenomenal time-trialling, while encouraging the climbers to attack in the high mountains. The result? Anquetil won the time trials, skinned the likes of Bahamontés for a stage win on the Tourmalet, and secured his fourth Tour on the 50th running of the race, by more than three and a half minutes.

OLDEST TOUR WINNERS

36 years, 4 months: Firmin Lambot (BEL) in 1922
34 years, 6 months: Henri Pélissier (FRA) in 1923
34 years, 0 months: Gino Bartali (ITA) in 1948
33 years, 11 months: Lance Armstrong (USA) in 2005
33 years, 7 months: Joop Zoetemelk (HOL) in 1980

1963: GEMINIANI'S CUTTING EDGE

If Anquetil's natural ability gave him the edge over his rivals, it was the excellence of the St-Raphaël-Gitane team that kept him ahead – in particular *directeur sportif* Raphaël Geminiani, a former Tour racer whose claim to fame was finishing second behind Hugo Koblet in 1951 (his other notable achievement was surviving the same bout of malaria that killed Fausto Coppi in 1960). When it came to protecting his man, Geminiani would stop at nothing. Never was this better illustrated than in 1963, during the mountain stage between Val-d'Isère and Chamonix, in which a rockfall meant the peloton was diverted up an unpaved goat track with sections of 18 per cent gradient. Geminiani realised that the gears on Anquetil's bike were not set up for such a severe climb. He also knew that Tour regulations allowed for no changes of equipment except after mechanical failure. While no one was looking, Geminiani instructed his mechanic to lean out of the team car and snap Anquetil's gear cable with a pair of wire cutters. The race *commissaire*, utterly fooled by the deception, allowed Anquetil to change bikes at the foot of the climb. The Frenchman soared up the track and onwards to an unlikely stage win in Chamonix, his faithful *directeur* as ever following close behind.

UNDERHAND TACTICS

When it comes to influencing the result of the Tour de France, all manner of devious cheating methods have been employed. They include:

Lifts: In the early years, riders would regularly grab a lift in supporters' cars or else cling to them. In 1928 two riders jumped in a taxi after the truck they were travelling in crashed into a ditch. In the 1990s some riders were found to be hooking their feed bags to the wing mirrors of their support cars for a free ride up a mountain.

Trees: In 1904 fans blocked the road with felled trees to prevent rival riders getting past.

Violence: As well as occasionally beating up riders, in 1904 a group of fans chased Maurice Garin and Lucien Pothier for 3.5 miles (6 km) in a car in an attempt to run them off the road.

Poison: Henri Cornet claimed to have been fed poisoned chicken in 1904; Paul Duboc was poisoned in 1911.

Sabotage: In 1910 Gustave Garrigou discovered his bike had been interfered with when the hub fell off and all the ball bearings spilled across the road; in 1937 Roger Lapébie was warming up when he noticed someone had sawed through his handlebars.

Short cuts: In 1906 three riders caught the train to Dijon, but were caught by Tour officials who happened to be at the station exit; three-times Tour winner Philippe Thys once asked a shepherd for a short cut over the Col du Peyresourde, but got lost on the goat track.

1963: GREEN AND YELLOW

Dublin-born Shay Elliott was the pioneer who blazed a trail for Irish greats such as Stephen Roche and Sean Kelly. In 1963, competing in his fifth Tour de France, Elliott won the stage in Roubaix to become the first Irishman to wear the yellow jersey. It was the highlight of his Tour career, although many observers thought he should have won more races than he actually did. Elliott, however, was concerned about securing his financial future – and in those days there was more money to be made by helping other, more high-profile riders to win than actually winning yourself.

1963: ANQUETIL FINALLY ACCEPTED

Anquetil's fourth Tour victory in 1963 was greeted with markedly more enthusiasm by the French fans than any of his previous wins. Why? Perhaps because they recognised that this time he was truly deserving of the credit. The organisers had done all they could to make the course Anquetil-proof, yet he still won. Short of clapping him in irons, there seemed no way of stopping him. Like all great sporting champions, Anquetil's dominance took the excitement of the unknown out of the event, but it was now impossible not to acknowledge his greatness.

'In many ways he is reminiscent of Manuel Fangio, the greatest racing driver ever known,' wrote one commentator. 'Taking risks only when necessary, avoiding mechanical breakdowns, contenting himself skilfully and intelligently with giving each challenger the response needed to silence him.'

☆ TOUR STARS WHO DIED IN 1963

Gustave Garrigou, aged 78: One of the great early pioneers of the Tour, Garrigou rode eight times between 1907 and 1914 – and finished all of them. Not only that, but he won in 1911 and never finished outside the top five in the rest. He was also the first rider to climb the rutted, potholed donkey track to the summit of the Tourmalet without once dismounting. 'It was our job,' he remarked towards the end of his life. 'The prizes, the intermediary prizes, the contracts. I was a professional. It was just life.'

TOUR TRIVIA

British television coverage of the Tour began in 1963 on ITV's *WideWorld of Sport*. The commentator was David Saunders, a cycling correspondent for the *Daily Telegraph*.

▲ LEGENDARY MOUNTAINS OF THE TOUR: COL DE TOURMALET

The Pyrenean giant (6939 ft; 2,115 m) was first included in the Tour in 1910 and Octave Lapize – whose statue stands at the summit – was the first man to reach the top. Since then the Tourmalet has become the most-visited of all the Tour mountains, making up a fearsome loop which includes the Aubisque and the climb to Luz-Ardiden. However, the ski station at La Mongie, near its summit, has been used on two occasions as a stage finish. In 1913, while descending the mountain, Eugène Christophe was forced to carry his bike 6 miles (10 km) to the nearest blacksmith's forge in order to fix its broken forks.

TOUR TRIVIA
The winner of the King of the Mountains has been the first man over the Tourmalet on sixteen occasions since World War Two.

1964: THE DUEL ON THE VOLCANO

The Duel of the Puy de Dôme is still regarded as one of the great defining moments of Tour history. Certainly none of the 500,000 spectators by the roadside, nor the millions watching the event live on television for the first time, would ever forget what they saw.

After years of rivalry, here, at last, were Raymond Poulidor and Jacques Anquetil literally shoulder to shoulder in search of Tour victory. The stage to the top of the extinct volcano was crucial to both men, and to the outcome of the race itself. Anquetil led by 56 seconds, but Poulidor knew that if he could beat his rival here, he could very well win the Tour. For more than 6 miles (10 km) the two men were locked together, often appearing to be leaning on each other as the 7.5 per cent gradient began to bite.

'We were side by side,' Poulidor recalled. 'I slowed down, he slowed down. I attacked, he responded. It was astounding. I never again felt as bad on a bike.'

As they neared the summit, Poulidor finally managed to inch away until a gap opened between them. When he finally crossed the finish line there was no sign of Anquetil behind him. Had his great rival cracked? Had he got off his bike? 'For a moment I really thought I had won the Tour,' he said. Then, like a yellow-jerseyed spectre, Anquetil came round the corner. Shattered, he had retained the lead by just 14 seconds. It would be enough to secure him a fifth victory. 'If he had taken the jersey from me that day I would have gone home,' Anquetil later admitted.

'My contracts won't increase if I win a sixth Tour. And if I fail, I have everything to lose.'

Jacques Anquetil explains why he wouldn't be taking part in the 1965 Tour

'You don't have to win a lot of races each year to keep your market value high. It's the big wins that count.'

Vittorio Adorni, Italian cyclist

☆ TOUR STARS BORN IN 1964

Djamolidine Abdoujaparov: A Russian sprinter and three-times points winner, known as the Tashkent Terror because of his no-holds-barred style.

Raúl Alcalá: One of only two Mexicans to have ridden the Tour, Alcalá won the white jersey of best young rider in 1987 and won stages in 1989 and 1990.

Bjarne Riis: A Danish rider who won the Tour in 1996 aged 32, and later went on to become the highly successful manager of the CSC Team.

☆ TOURS STARS WHO DIED IN 1964

Honoré Barthélémy, aged 74: With just three finishes out of seven attempts in the 1920s, Barthélémy was not one of the Tour greats, but he became a legend due to a tragic incident in 1920 when he crashed during a stage and was blinded in one eye by a piece of flint. Remarkably, he finished eighth – but later lost the eye and replaced it with a glass one, which had an unfortunate habit of falling out during races.

In 1921, after winning a stage in Strasbourg, he was clapped on the back so vigorously that the eye shot out and he, along with several dozen spectators, were forced to get on their hands and knees to look for it. He later said, 'I spend all of the prize money I win on buying new eyes for the ones I lose in races!'

Hugo Koblet, aged 39: Swiss-born Koblet won the Tour on his first attempt in 1951, but health problems meant his career nosedived almost immediately and he failed to finish his subsequent attempts in 1953 and 1954. Indeed, he is best remembered as the playboy of the peloton, a man who carried eau de cologne and a sponge in his jersey pocket and who thought nothing of sitting up from the handlebars to comb his hair during a stage. In 1964 he was killed when his Alfa-Romeo smashed into a tree outside Zurich at 74 mph (120 kph). At the time his death was rumoured to be suicide brought about by debts and the disintegration of his marriage, although this was never proven.

Fermin Lambot, aged 77: This Belgian rider competed in ten Tours between 1911 and 1924, winning in 1919 – largely due to Eugène Christophe's broken forks – and in 1922, thanks to mechanical problems yet again wiping out Christophe and a time penalty thwarting Hector Heusghem.

TOUR TRIVIA
The peloton gets through 35,000 drinking bottles (*bidons*) during the three weeks of the Tour.

MOUNTAIN CATEGORIES

All hills and mountains on the Tour are assigned a category from one to four, which describes their difficulty. The toughest mountains are described as 'Hors Catégorie', meaning an altitude difference of more than 3,280 ft (1,000 m) and an average gradient of 7 per cent or greater.

The categories are decided according to the following criteria:
- length of the climb
- altitude difference from bottom to top
- average (and steepest) grade
- summit elevation
- climb's position on the stage (early or late)
- width and conditions of the road

Typically for the Tour, Category Four is an easy, short climb, Category Three is the easiest 'real' climb – ie, 3 miles (5 km) at a 5 per cent gradient, Category Two is approximately 3 miles at a gradient of 8 to 8.5 per cent; while Category One is a long climb 9–12 miles (15–20 km) or more at 5 to 6 per cent.

1965: POU-POU KAPUT

Could 1965 be Poulidor's year? Certainly he would never have a better chance of winning the Tour. Not only was he in the best form of his life, but Anquetil wasn't racing and of the other potential winners only Bahamontés stood out and he was now 37 years old. It was now or never for Pou-Pou – but once again he was to be thwarted. This time the winner was a 22-year-old Italian called Felice Gimondi, who came from nowhere to snatch the *maillot jaune* on stage four with a lead of three minutes and, apart from two stages, kept it all the way to Paris. Those who had dared to criticise Poulidor for tactical failings in the past had yet more evidence that it was this, rather than luck, which had contributed to his lack of Tour success. Still, he fought back in the belief that by winning the final mountain time trial up the 5,000 ft (1,537 m) Mont Revard he would finally smash the hoodoo. On the day it was Gimondi who smashed Poulidor, beating him by 33 seconds. A star was born. Pou-Pou couldn't believe it.

TOUR TRIVIA
Felice Gimondi, at 22, was the youngest post-war winner of the Tour de France.

☆ TOUR STARS WHO DIED IN 1965

Maurice Brocco, aged 82: Not exactly a legend of the event, having failed to complete any of the six Tours he entered between 1908 and 1914, but Brocco is the man for whom the term *domestique* was coined by the disgusted Henri Desgrange after the French rider let it be known he was amenable to bribes from other riders for his service during the race.

Odile Defraye: The first Belgian to win the Tour in 1912 – the only Tour of the seven he started between 1909 and 1924 that he actually finished.

1966: DRUG DISPUTE

In 1965 tests in Belgium concluded that 37 per cent of professional cyclists used some form of performance-enhancing drugs. It came as a surprise to no one. The only surprise came the following year when, after more than 60 years of turning a blind eye to the problem, the Tour de France introduced mandatory drug testing. The reaction from the riders was one of outrage, especially when doctors and police officers burst into their rooms on the eve of the Bordeaux to Bayonne stage in order to carry out the tests. The next day, the riders – led by Jacques Anquetil – dismounted from their bikes in protest. It was the first time drug testing had brought the Tour to a standstill, and it would not be the last.

1966: SIMPSON'S SAFER DRUGS

Anquetil had always been matter-of-fact when it came to drug use. When Tom Simpson died on the Ventoux in 1967, the Frenchman claimed that the culture of drug testing meant Simpson could no longer use the 'safer' drugs that he had been used to. Drugs or no drugs, Anquetil himself was facing up to the one adversary that was guaranteed to beat him: time. In 1966, at the age of 32 and having claimed he would never ride the Tour again, Maître Jacques set off for one last hurrah. Sadly, he would be mainly remembered in this particular edition of the Tour for leading a protest against the introduction of doping controls. In the saddle, a combination of weariness and bronchitis took its toll; he was already well out of contention when his old rival Poulidor beat him in a time trial by seven seconds. For a while he devoted himself to the service of team-mate and eventual winner Lucien Aimar, but on stage nineteen to St Etienne, Anquetil stopped, and with millions watching on live TV, combed his hair and stepped into the broom wagon. An era had come to an end.

1966: THE NOWHERE MAN

Lucien Aimar won the 1966 Tour despite not winning a stage. In fact, he won only one stage in the ten Tours in which he competed. In his entire career he won only three big races and has, as a result, been described as one of the 'more forgettable' Tour winners.

TOUR TRIVIA

Tommaso de Pra of Italy was naturally jubilant after winning the stage between Bayonne and Pau in 1966 after a solo breakaway. It was only afterwards he discovered the reason he'd got away was that, unknown to him, the rest of the field had staged a ten-minute go-slow protest behind him as part of the rumbling dispute over drug testing.

☆ TOUR STARS WHO DIED IN 1966

Sylvère Maes, aged 57: A Belgian rider who won the 1936 Tour a year after it had been won by fellow countryman – but no relation – Romain Maes. He won again in 1939.

TOUR TRIVIA

In 1967, English amateur Arthur Metcalfe rode the Tour during a three-week holiday from work at an insurance firm in Leeds. He finished 69th, and returned again the following year after getting permission from his boss.

1967: THE DEATH OF MR TOM

With Anquetil gone at last, a number of riders fancied their chances at Tour glory in 1967. There was Poulidor, inevitably, and Gimondi was lurking, as was the previous year's winner Aimar. For the first time, though, a British rider could justifiably count himself among one of the pre-race favourites.

Having arrived in Europe in 1962, Tom Simpson had made an instant impression both with his riding ability and his larger-than-life personality. The French media loved him; they called him 'Mr Tom' and loved to set up stunts in which he paraded around Paris in a bowler hat. Simpson, unlike almost every British pro before him, fitted right in with the continental lifestyle. He learned the language and the customs of the people, and, more importantly, he earned the respect of the peloton. Between 1963 and 1966 he won the legendary Bordeaux–Paris and Milan–San Remo classics, and the World Championship in 1965. Tour de France success continued to elude him, however. Although he finished sixth in 1962, having become the first Englishman to wear the yellow jersey, his subsequent record was patchy. He did not compete in 1963, in 1964 he was fourteenth, while in 1965 and 1966 he did not finish. In 1967, at the age of 30 and with pressure to impress potential sponsors weighing on his mind, Simpson planned his assault on the Tour carefully.

After much consideration he decided to target the stage between Marseille and Carpentras, which crossed the iconic moonscape of the

Vive le Tour!

Ventoux. In temperatures nudging 130°F (54°C), it was soon clear that Simpson was in trouble.

'He was riding like an amateur, zig-zagging all over the place,' recalled his mechanic Harry Hall. When Simpson eventually crashed into the roadside, Hall was first on the scene. 'That's it for you, Tom,' he said – but Simpson insisted on continuing. Legend has it that his last words were, 'Put me back on my bike'. A few yards further up the road, Simpson collapsed again. Despite the immediate attention of the Tour doctor Pierre Dumas, it was too late. By the time he was helicoptered off the mountain he was most probably already dead, although the official announcement did not come until 5.40 pm that evening.

The cause of death was given as heart collapse from heat and overwork. Sadly, it was no great shock when the post-mortem examination revealed Simpson's blood was filled with drugs. His use of amphetamine was well known in the peloton, and this time it seemed that in his desire for victory he had gone too far.

Today, a monument stands on the spot where Simpson died. On the 30th anniversary of his death, a plaque was added which reads, 'There is no mountain too high. Your daughters Jane and Joanne, 13 July 1997.'

'It is like another world up there among the bare rocks and the glaring sun. The white rocks reflect the heat and the dust rises clinging to your arms, legs and face. I rode well up there doing about five miles to the gallon in perspiration. It was almost overwhelmingly hot up there and I think it is the only time that I have got off my bike and my pants have nearly fallen down. They were soaked and heavy with sweat which was running off me in streams and I had to wring out my socks because the sweat was running into my shoes.'

Tom Simpson describes an earlier ride over Mont Ventoux

'We often asked ourselves if this athlete, who at work often appeared in pain, had not committed some errors in the way he looked after himself.'

Tour director **Jacques Goddet's** thinly-disguised criticism of Tom Simpson's drug use

'Simpson's case comes at a time when all the legal, moral, spiritual and scientific communities need to join forces to restore the moral order. But today, let us weep for Tom Simpson, a decent chap who probably simply feared defeat.'

Editorial in *L'Équipe* on the day Simpson died

1967: A SALUTARY VICTORY

The day after Tom Simpson's death the remaining members of his Great Britain team – Vin Denson, Barry Hoban and Colin Lewis – wore black armbands. Race favourite Felice Gimondi was in tears. The stage from Carpentras to Sète was a sombre affair, which the Tour dedicated to Simpson. First over the line was Barry Hoban – although few statistics have ever been rendered so unimportant by events.

TOUR TRIVIA
Barry Hoban, who rode in twelve Tours, eventually married Helen Simpson, the widow of Tom Simpson.

Vive le Tour!

TOUR TRIVIA

Lucien Aimar was fined £50 a day during the 1967 Tour for refusing to wear the jersey of French national champion. He was protesting that Desire Letort, who had won the race, was subsequently disqualified for doping offences.

1967: PINGEON PULLS IT OFF

Tom Simpson's death on the Ventoux overshadowed a fine Tour victory for Frenchman Roger Pingeon, ironically a team-mate of Simpson's at Peugeot. The victory was established as early as stage five, when Pingeon secured the yellow jersey with a spectacular 37.5 mile (60 km) solo breakaway that gained him a lead of six minutes.

TOUR TRIVIA

After every stage, Roger Pingeon bathed in diluted vinegar and salt solution to kill the germs which he believed could ruin his chances of winning the Tour. He also believed in sleeping in complete darkness, wearing eye masks and even stuffing the keyholes of his hotel room with cotton wool to stop the light coming in.

1967: POULIDOR'S WOES CONTINUE

The gallant Raymond Poulidor's Tour once again ended in catastrophe when, after falling on a mountain descent, he was forced to wait several minutes for the support vehicle, which had broken down. By the time he got going again – on a spare bike that didn't fit him properly – he was eleven minutes behind the stage winner and once again out of the Tour.

1968: TOUR BORE

Following Tom Simpson's death and the drug furore that surrounded it, the organisers declared the 1968 event *le Tour de la Santé* – the Tour of Health – and arranged for the *Grand Départ* to take place at the spa town of Vittel. Unfortunately, journalists soon dubbed it *le Tour de Sommeil* – the Tour of Sleep – due to the unimaginative stages that led to a host of bunched finishes. When organiser Felix Levitan accused the press of watching the race through 'stale eyes', the reporters responded by going on strike for one stage.

1968: NOSE TROUBLE

The Tour trials and tribulations of Raymond Poulidor were, by 1968, becoming something of a standing joke. It was now not a question of whether Pou-Pou would win the Tour, but how he would lose it. Sure enough, his Tour that year ended when he was knocked off his bike by a motorcycle outrider, suffering a fractured nose in the process.

TOUR TRIVIA

Franco Bitossi, the Italian sprinter who finished a highly creditable eighth in the 1968 Tour, had a heart condition that occasionally caused him to be immobilised in the middle of races. It was this, as well as his eyeballs-out style, that earned him the nickname *Cuore Mato* – 'Mad Heart'.

KINGS OF THE MOUNTAIN

Victories

7: Richard Virenque (FRA) – 1994, 1995, 1996, 1997, 1999, 2003, 2004
6: Lucien Van Impe (BEL) – 1971, 1972, 1975, 1977, 1981, 1983
6: Federico Bahamontés (SPA) – 1954, 1958, 1959, 1962, 1963, 1964
3: Julio Jiménez (SPA) – 1965, 1966, 1967

Victories by nation

18: France
15: Spain
12: Italy
11: Belgium
3: Columbia
2: Luxembourg, Netherlands
1: Great Britain, Switzerland

1968: HERMAN'S HORROR SHOW

Leading the field by 16 seconds, all Belgium's Herman van Springel had
to do in order to win his first Tour de France was survive the final time
trial, a 34 mile (55.2 km) sprint from Melun to Paris. The occasion,
though, proved too much for him and he choked, allowing the relatively
unknown Jan Janssen to spring from nowhere to win by 38 seconds and
become the first Dutchman to win the Tour.

☆ TOUR STARS BORN IN 1968

Laurent Jalabert: one of the modern greats of French cycling, who competed in eleven Tours between 1991 and 2002, winning the green 'points'-jersey twice and the King of the Mountains twice as well. The latter was a particularly impressive achievement, as Jalabert suffered from altitude sickness whenever he went over 4,900 ft (1,500 m).

TOUR WINNERS 1961–1968

1961: Jacques Anquetil (FRA), [KoM: Imerio Massignan (ITA); Points: André Darrigade (FRA)]

1962: Jacques Anquetil (FRA), [KoM: Federico Bahamontés (SPA); Points: Rudi Altig (FDR)]

1963: Jacques Anquetil (FRA), [KoM: Federico Bahamontés (SPA); Points: Rik Van Looy (BEL)]

1964: Jacques Anquetil (FRA), [KoM: Federico Bahamontés (SPA); Points: Jan Janssen (NED)]

1965: Felice Gimondi (ITA), [KoM: Julio Jiménez (SPA); Points: Jan Janssen (NED)]

1966: Lucien Aimar (FRA), [KoM: Julio Jiménez (SPA); Points: Willy Plankaert (BEL)]

Vive le Tour!

1967: Roger Pingeon (FRA), [KoM: Julio Jiménez (SPA); Points: Jan Janssen (NED)]

1968: Jan Janssen (NED), [KoM: Aurelio González (SPA); Points: Franco Bitossi (ITA)]

THE CANNIBAL AND THE BADGER 1969–1980

'Nothing can ever compare to this. There will only ever be one Eddy Merckx in the history of cycling. He is a mystery of human creation.'

L'Équipe

ANATOMY OF A LEGEND: EDDY MERCKX

Edouard Louis Joseph Merckx was born in Meensel-Kiezegem, Belgium, on 17 June 1945. He first started competitive riding aged 19 in 1961. At 19 he was World Amateur Champion. Before his Tour debut aged 25 in 1969, he had won the Giro d'Italia, three Milan–San Remos, two Ghent–Wevelgems, the Tour of Flanders, the Flèche Wallonne, the Paris–Roubaix, and the World Championship.

In 1972 Merckx broke the world hour record when he rode 30.71 miles (49.43 km) at altitude in Mexico City, a feat that stood until 1984.

Despite his phenomenal stamina, Merckx was a heavy smoker and once advertised cigarettes in a TV commercial.

A station on the Brussels Metro is named after him, and the bike on which he broke the world hour record is on display there.

Merckx won the equivalent of a race a week for six years. One which eluded him, however, was the prestigious Paris–Tours classic. Fellow

Belgian Noel Van Tyghem, who did win the race, once claimed, 'Between us, me and Eddy Merckx won every classic that can be won. I won Paris–Tours, Merckx won all the rest.'

Merckx's son Axel, born in 1972, is also a professional bike rider. When he won a stage of the 2000 Giro d'Italia, Merckx senior broke down in tears in the commentary box.

After retiring in 1979, Merckx set up a highly successful bike manufacturing business. In 1996 he was given the ceremonial title 'Baron' by the King of Belgium, and in 2000 he was chosen as Belgium's 'Sports Figure of the Century'.

1969: MERCKX – THE CHAMPION WAITING TO HAPPEN

It wasn't as if the Tour hadn't been forewarned about what was about to happen. Even so, the way in which the 25-year-old Eddy Merckx destroyed the field in his debut Tour in 1969 left the sport reeling and his rivals psychologically shot. He was, quite simply, unstoppable. On the flat and in the mountains, Merckx produced a performance that was utterly dominant. He not only won the *maillot jaune*, but the 'points' jersey and the King of the Mountains prize. The highlight was an astonishing solo break of 81 miles (130 km) over the Tourmalet while already wearing yellow and with the Tour in the bag. '*Merckxissimo!*' exclaimed Tour director Jacques Goddet. The riders, however, were already calling him by the more sinister nickname, '*Cannibal!*'

TOUR TRIVIA

Romain Maes, the last Belgian winner of the Tour in 1935, was one of the first to greet Merckx at the end of his victorious 1969 Tour.

'Over the whole 130 km we witnessed a sad, gloomy march of resigned men, totally demoralised by the cruel nature of the situation . . . It was not an attitude to be proud of, but perhaps we can sympathise with the disillusionment of these men, aware of their relative inadequacy in the face of such fundamental genius . . . Never again will we be able to say that the Tour is not won until Paris. Eddy Merckx has destroyed that legend too.'

L'Équipe

THE CLOSEST TOUR FINISHES

Year	Riders	Time difference
1989:	Greg Lemond – Laurent Fignon	0.08 seconds
1968:	Jan Janssen – Herman van Springel	0.38
1987:	Stephen Roche – Pedro Delgado	0.40
1977:	Bernard Thévenet – Hennie Kuiper	0.48
1964:	Jacques Anquetil – Raymond Poulidor	0.55
1933:	Georges Speicher – Learco Guerra	1 minute 01 second
1966:	Lucien Aimar – Jan Janssen	1.07
1956:	Roger Walkowiak – Gilbert Bauvin	1.25
1996:	Bjarne Riis – Jan Ullrich	1.41
1985:	Bernard Hinault – Greg Lemond	1.42

1969: THE CANNIBAL'S REVENGE

Just why did Eddy Merckx seek to dominate every aspect of the 1969 Tour? One possible reason is revenge. Earlier that year he had been unceremoniously booted out of the Giro d'Italia on what looked like suspiciously trumped-up doping charges. To this day Merckx protests his innocence, and has always regarded the stain on his reputation as the result of foreign resentment at his dominance over 'their' event.

BACK IN THE SADDLE

Merckx was renowned as a perfectionist. He always carried a spanner in his back pocket so that he could adjust the saddle or handlebars on his bike mid-race if necessary. In fact, having the correct height and angle was vital in order for Merckx to ride at all. In 1969, shortly after the Tour, he was involved in a horrific crash on an indoor track which left his motorcycle pacer dead and the Belgian with serious back and pelvic injuries. From that moment on, he was always in discomfort – especially on the climbs – and without minute adjustments to his position on the bike he would have found it impossible to compete. 'Before the accident climbing was a pleasure,' he said. 'Now it is a torment.'

A GLORIOUS CAREER

A glance at Eddy Merckx's cycling achievements gives some indication of just how he dominated the sport.

- Five-times champion of both the Tour de France and the Giro d'Italia
- Only one of four cyclists to have won the Tour, the Giro and the Vuelta
- Only one of two men to have won the Triple Crown of Cycling – Tour, Giro, and World Championship – in the same year

- Winner of all five Monument races (the classics: Milan–San Remo, Tour of Flanders, Paris–Roubaix, Liège–Bastogne–Liège, Tour of Lombardy)
- Winner of 525 of the 1,582 races he took part in during his career

TOUR TRIVIA

The Belgian government was so delighted with Merckx's win, they announced a national holiday in his honour.

☆ TOUR STARS BORN IN 1969

Richard Virenque: He was the darling of French cycling fans who won seven King of the Mountains jerseys between 1994 and 2004, but whose copybook was irreversibly blotted by his involvement in the Festina Affair of 1998 and his subsequent admission of drug-taking.

☆ TOUR STARS WHO DIED IN 1969

Léon Scieur, aged 81: A Belgian rider who won the Tour in 1921.

1970: MERCKX RELENTLESS AGAIN

In 1970 Merckx set about the Tour with the same relentless power and efficiency as the previous year, and with the same result. This time, the killer stage was the one that finished at the summit of Mont Ventoux, included for the first time since Tom Simpson's death. Here, in equally suffocating heat, Merckx simply blew the peloton apart. As he passed Simpson's memorial, he removed his cap in respect before powering up the remaining 1.8 miles (3 km) of the climb on his own. At the summit, however, the effort of winning in such extreme conditions became plain when the Belgian fainted and had to be given oxygen.

☆ TOUR STARS BORN IN 1970

Erik Zabel: Eleven Tours between 1995 and 2006 brought East German-born Erik Zabel six green 'points' jerseys and made him the pre-eminent sprinter of his era. Ferociously competitive, he postponed his planned retirement at the end of the 2006 season after narrowly failing to win the World Championship. Zabel now plans to ride in the 2007 Tour during which he will turn 37 years old.

THE PEUGEOT TEAM

Peugeot was one of the most famous teams of the 1960s and 1970s, with one of the most distinctive shirt designs. Among the legendary riders to wear the Peugeot shirt were Eddy Merckx and Britain's Tom Simpson.

☆ TOUR STARS WHO DIED IN 1970

Eugène Christophe, aged 85: The first rider to wear the *maillot jaune* in 1919, he was perhaps better known for walking 6 miles (10 km) down the Tourmalet with a broken bike in search of a blacksmith in 1913 (see F****** Forks!, page 22).

1971: THE AGONY OF OCAÑA

If there was one rider who even came close to equalling Eddy Merckx in his pomp, it was the Spaniard Luis Ocaña. In 1969 a heavy fall in the mountains put him out of contention, and the following year he was beset with illness. In 1971, however, he set about giving Merckx his sternest challenge yet. Up until the Alps, it had been pretty much business as usual for the Belgian. But on the road to Orcieres-Merlette on stage eleven, Ocaña flew up the climbs and took the yellow jersey by nine minutes from a strangely subdued Merckx. The next day, Merckx fought back furiously – but despite winning the stage, he could only claw back two minutes on the Spaniard. Could it be that the Cannibal had met his match? We will never know for sure. The race was decided on the Pyrenean stage from Revel to Luchon. Merckx attacked. Ocaña gave chase. A storm erupted, and soon the roads were slithery with mud. Merckx crashed on the perilous descent of the Col de Mente, but managed to scramble back onto his bike. Ocaña skidded out of control on a corner, and was not so lucky. As he climbed to his feet, Joop Zoetemelk smashed into him at high speed. Ocaña sprawled to the ground, his face a mask of agony, his Tour over. At the stage finish, a clearly distraught Merckx refused to wear the yellow jersey and even considered quitting the race altogether. 'Whatever happens I have lost the Tour,' he said. 'The doubt will always remain.'

'Given the lead that Luis Ocaña has, I don't see how, at the moment, the Tour de France could possibly slip through his fingers. It's virtually impossible for me to make up my deficit, unless I find new strength from somewhere or unless he performs very badly. But I don't want to think about that. I don't believe it will happen.'

Vive le Tour!

Eddy Merckx on the eve of the crash which put Luis Ocaña out of
the 1971 Tour

TOUR TRIVIA

Riders called to give dope tests must give a urine sample within 35
minutes of their appearance on the podium. Dehydration can often
make this a lengthy process.

☆ TOUR STARS BORN IN 1971

Lance Armstrong: The greatest rider ever? Or one who devalued the
sport by concentrating solely on the Tour de France? What cannot be
disputed is that the Texan beat life-threatening cancer to win an
unprecedented seven consecutive Tours.

☆ TOUR STARS WHO DIED IN 1971

Shay Elliott, aged 38: Elliott was the first great Irish cyclist in Europe, the man who became the first from the Emerald Isle to wear the yellow jersey in 1963 (see Green and Yellow, see page 108). Sadly it was to be the highlight of an unfulfilled career. Dogged by financial problems, Elliott burned his boats with professional cycling when he accepted money from a tabloid newspaper to spill the beans about drug use in the *peloton*. In April 1971, facing bankruptcy, he shot himself in the head with a shotgun in his garage in Dublin.

Philippe Thys, aged 80: The legendary Belgian rider who became the first to win the Tour on three occasions, in 1913, 1914 and, remarkably, in 1920 after being accused of being overweight and arrogant by Henri Desgrange (see Anatomy of a Legend: Philippe Thys, page 3).

1972: CHAIR LIFT FOR CYRIL

The 1972 Tour was billed as a rematch between Merckx and Ocaña, but it was sprinter Cyril Guimard of France who was wearing yellow at the end of stage eight. Unfortunately, Guimard was in so much pain from a knee injury that he had to be carried to the start on a chair. He quit the race in tears, and was in tears again in Paris when Merckx symbolically handed him the green jersey of the points winner.

1972: OCAÑA CRASHES OUT AGAIN

The much-anticipated Merckx–Ocaña clash – hyped up with some barbed words between the two riders in the weeks leading up to the Tour – failed to materialise, and once again it was a high-speed crash that did for the Spaniard. Desperately chasing Merckx on a rain-lashed Pyrenean descent, Ocaña, Bernard Thévenet of France and Lucien Van Impe of Belgium came round a corner only to find a line of cars blocking their way. The resulting crash left Ocaña covered in blood and more than a minute behind Merckx. He abandoned the race soon after with a lung infection, but in truth his confidence and his morale had been shot to pieces by the second major crash in successive years.

TOUR TRIVIA

Luis Ocaña was the first rider to use titanium for the headset and bottom bracket of his bike.

☆ TOUR STARS BORN IN 1972

Robbie McEwen: Known as the Pocket Rocket, former BMX champion McEwen has become one of the most successful Australian riders in the Tour, winning three green 'points' Jerseys in 2002, 2004 and 2006 and eleven sprint finishes, including victory on the Champs Élysées in 1999.

1973: IF AT FIRST YOU DON'T SUCCEED…

Having completed a historic double by winning the Giro and the Vuelta in the spring, Eddy Merckx was entitled to a rest from the Tour de France in 1973. For Luis Ocaña, here was surely the chance he had been waiting for after three years of unremitting bad luck. When, on stage two, he crashed after a dog ran across the road in front of him, the Spaniard must have thought he was cursed. Fortunately, he was not seriously injured and by stage seven was wearing yellow. He would not relinquish it for the rest of the Tour, and there were few observers – not even Merckx – who could begrudge him his long-awaited victory.

INDUSTRIAL ACTION

The peloton has been compared to a trade union. And like a trade union, its shop stewards are not averse to calling their members out on strike over grievances. Here is a round-up of cycling's industrial actions.

1905: The first stage is disrupted by saboteurs scattering nails and other debris on the road, resulting in all but fifteen riders failing to reach the finish within the time limit. When Henri Desgrange threatens to disqualify them anyway, a strike is called. Desgrange quickly changes his mind, allowing the latecomers to continue but docking them points nevertheless.

1920: Once again Desgrange's autocratic style causes friction, as more than half the riders down tools in protest at the length of the stages and the merciless rules. An unrepentant Desgrange responds by accusing them of being shirkers afraid of physical work.

1921: Henri Pélissier takes exception to the edict that all riders must use identical *musettes*, or food bags. He claims all riders have different requirements, and goes on strike.

1925: Pélissier, along with his brother Francis, form the first and only

Vive le Tour!

official cyclists' union and immediately calls for industrial action. Once again the bone of contention is the standard *musette*. Unfortunately for Pélissier, he is so universally unpopular among the other riders that the strike collapses, and with it the union.

1966: Rumours of an impending drugs raid lead to riders fleeing their hotel rooms. The only rider left is the ever-popular Raymond Poulidor, who is duly tested. Furious at what they claim is an infringement of their liberties, the peloton climb off their bikes a few kilometres into the following day's stage. Feelings are still running high the following day, when a go-slow is called.

1978: Annoyed at the number of lengthy transfers between stages, the resulting early starts, and the concept of split stages, the peloton climbs off at Valence d'Agen. Tour organiser Jacques Goddet agrees to scrap split stages in the future.

1990: The peloton strike when the Tour organisers refuse to disqualify renowned doper Gert-Jan Theunisse after the Belgian is caught cheating on two occasions but reprieved because of a 'technical error'.

1991: When Urs Zimmerman is disqualified for driving to the next stage start instead of getting a plane transfer, the peloton goes on strike. Zimmerman is reinstated after explaining that he is scared of flying.

1998: In protest at the police raids resulting from the Festina Affair, the riders sit in the road at the start of a stage.

1973: WAITING FOR GODDET

Aged 37, Raymond Poulidor was no longer considered a potential Tour winner. But this did not stop him competing – and nor did it stop his catalogue of calamities. While descending the Portet d'Aspet in the Pyrenees, Pou-Pou misjudged a tight bend and went flying into a ravine. He was eventually helped out by race director Jacques Goddet, but once again his Tour was over.

TOUR TRIVIA

Luis Ocaña was the toast of Spain following his 1973 Tour win, but the feeling was not mutual. Indeed, Ocaña always claimed that one of his main motivations was to avenge his father's exile by General Franco's fascist regime.

TOUR TRIVIA

It's a tradition at the top of mountains for spectators to hand the riders newspapers to stuff down their jerseys to keep them warm during the high-speed and often freezing-cold descents.

☆ TOUR STARS BORN IN 1973

Joseba Beloki: A Spanish rider who between 2000 and 2002 came third twice and second once, largely by sticking limpet-like to the leaders, but whose career came to a juddering halt after a horrific crash on the stage into Gap in 2003. His next Tour appearance was in 2005 when he finished 75th. The following year he was withdrawn on the eve of the race after being implicated in the Operation Puerto anti-drugs bust (see Operation Puerto, page 247).

Jan Ullrich: A red-haired German rider schooled within the East German sporting system, Ullrich won the Tour aged 23 in 1997 and was regarded as the next big thing (see Jan the Man, page 205); but found himself the eternal bridesmaid to Lance Armstrong in the years that followed. Regarded as one of the finest natural bike riders in the peloton, Ullrich had a constant struggle with his weight and often turned up to the Tour looking decidedly podgy. He was also renowned for his partying – crashing his Porsche into a rack of bikes on one occasion, and being found with amphetamine in his system after a night out on another. In 2006, with Armstrong retired, Ullrich was hot favourite to end his own career with a second Tour win. But he, along with several other top riders, was thrown out of the Tour after Operation Puerto became public knowledge (see Operation Puerto). He was subsequently sacked by his Telekom team, and at the age of 34 his career looks to be permanently over.

THE TOUR'S FASTEST STAGES

Stage: 50.355 kph; Laval–Blois (191 km) in 1999, won by Mario Cipollini (ITA)

Individual Time Trial: 54.545 kph: Versailles–Paris (24 km) in 1989, won by Greg Lemond (USA)

Prologue: 55152 kph: Lille–Lille (7.2 km) in 1994, won by Chris Boardman (GBR)

1974: THE BLOODY TOUR

There is no other sporting event that is as gruelling as the Tour de France, so one can only imagine the torment Eddy Merckx must have gone through in 1974 when he not only completed but won the Tour after undergoing an operation on his perineum. 'After the Prologue the lining on my shorts was soaked in blood,' he said. 'It was to stay that way for the duration of the Tour.'

1974: TOUR DE PLYMPTON BYPASS

There is much excitement about the *Grand Départ* from Britain in 2007, and quite rightly so. With an exciting Prologue through the streets of central London and a challenging stage through Kent, the British leg of the Tour promises to be as enthusiastically followed as any in France. It was not always so, however. In 1972 the Tour organisers grandly announced that stage three of the 1974 race would be staged along the south coast of England. What transpired was one of the most boring stages in Tour history. The police were unwilling to block off the roads, which meant the majority of the 101 mile (163 km) route was confined to going up and down the newly built, yet-to-be-opened, and wholly unscenic, Plympton bypass near Plymouth. There were fewer than expected spectators lining the verges, and the racing was little more than a high-speed procession that was eventually won by the unknown Henrik Poppe of Holland. The sarcastic headline in one English newspaper the next day read: *Tour de France – Can 40 Million Frenchmen Be Wrong?* Hardly surprising, then, that it would be another twenty years before the Tour returned to British shores.

1974: MERCKX UNSTOPPABLE

With Ocaña missing due to a contractual dispute with his employers, and Joop Zoetemelk injured, the 1974 Tour win – his record-equalling fifth – was perhaps Eddy Merckx's easiest. In fact, were it not for the exploits of the evergreen Raymond Poulidor it may well have rated as one of the most boring races of all time. Instead, the 38-year-old startled everyone by dropping Merckx and the rest of the peloton on Mont du Chat, during a mountain stage of the Alps, and winning a stage in the Pyrenees to finish the Eternal Second once again. But these were just brief flickers of excitement in a Tour in which Merckx won eight stages, giving him a new record of 32 wins and surpassing the previous record of 25 belonging to André Leducq.

'I have known a few champions, men like Coppi, Van Looy and Altig, but none of them could have dropped the entire peloton like Merckx did today. On the other hand, it is not acceptable for the peloton to surrender like that. There must be riders out there lacking in self-esteem.'

Jacques Anquetil comments on another Merckx solo break during the 1974 Tour

1975: I EAT CANNIBAL

For nearly a decade it had seemed impossible, but on the morning of 14 July 1975 the world woke up to the news that Eddy Merckx was indeed human. The previous day, on stage fifteen of the Tour de France, the Cannibal was finally skewered in the event he had made his own, after being unceremoniously dropped on an Alpine climb. Merckx could only watch as first Felice Gimondi and then Frenchman Bernard Thévenet shot past him on the climb to Pra-Loup. Thévenet grabbed the *maillot jaune* at the summit, but what nobody suspected was that Merckx had worn the yellow jersey for the last time in his illustrious career.

'Merckx is beaten! The Bastille has fallen!'

A sign on the road in 1975

1975: SUCKER PUNCH

Merckx's dramatic crack-up on the climb to Pra-Loup can be traced back to an incident two days earlier on the Puy de Dôme. It was here in 1964 that Jacques Anquetil and Raymond Poulidor had fought their great duel, one of the great moments in Tour history (see The Duel on the Volcano, page 110). Now the slopes of the extinct volcano were the scene of one of the event's most shameful chapters. Merckx, chasing his record sixth Tour, was pursuing Thévenet to the summit when a French spectator lunged from the roadside and smashed his fist into the Belgian's kidneys. Barely able to breath with pain, Merckx somehow managed to finish the stage losing less than a minute to his rivals. But it was clear he was in distress, and despite – or perhaps because of – a course of blood-thinning medication he was a shadow of himself when the race resumed after the rest day. Incredibly, two days later, Merckx was involved in a collision with Denmark's Ole Ritter and fractured his jaw. Yet it is a mark of the man that, although his chances of winning were gone, he refused to abandon the race, knowing that it would devalue Bernard Thévenet's inevitable victory.

LEGENDARY TOUR MOUNTAINS: COL D'ISERAN

At a whopping 9,088 ft (2,770 m) the Iseran is the highest of the mountain summit finishes used by the Tour. As a result, it is often afflicted by horrendous weather conditions. In 1996 the race had to be rerouted because of snow blocking the pass – which turned out to be hugely advantageous to Bjarne Riis (See The Riis Stuff, page 200). Although not particularly steep – the gradient rarely reaches 5 per cent – the climb is 24 miles (40 km) long, and passes through twelve unlit tunnels. The first man over the summit was Belgium's Félicien Vervaecke in 1938. The Iseran was also used for the Tour's first mountain time trial the following year, when Sylvère Maes made it a Belgian double.

TOUR TRIVIA

One small consolation for Eddy Merckx was that after being punched by a spectator on the Puy de Dôme, he recognised his assailant at the summit and was able to point him out to police officers who duly arrested him.

1975: WRONG TURN

The Bianchi team manager Giancarlo Ferretti had a lucky escape in 1975 when, while attempting to overtake parked press cars on the Col d'Allos, his car smashed through safety barriers and plunged nearly 500 ft (150 m) into a ravine. Ferretti suffered only minor injuries, as did the team mechanic who was a passenger in the car.

🏔 LEGENDARY MOUNTAINS OF THE TOUR: CROIX DE FER

With a gradient of just 4.7 per cent, the Croix de Fer is one of the more gentle ascents in the Alps. However, the climb goes on for a numbing 19.5 miles (31.5 km) to a summit 6,785ft (2,068 m) above sea level. It was first climbed by the Tour in 1947, and the first rider to the top was the Italian Fermo Camellini.

☆ TOUR STARS BORN IN 1975

Magnus Backstedt: The amiable Swede is the biggest rider in the current peloton, standing 6ft 3 ins (1.93 m) and weighing in at 14 stone (90 kg). He was the first man from Sweden to win a stage of the Tour in 1998. He lives and trains in South Wales (see The Pisspot Rebellion, page 227).

Floyd Landis: The winner of the 2006 Tour, which included a sensational 74 mile (120 km) solo breakaway. The title now in dispute after he was found to have illegal amounts of testosterone in his bloodstream (see What a Dope, page 250).

1976: FRENCH DESPAIR

Beaten in the 1975 Tour de France, Eddy Merckx's subsequent eighth place in the 1976 Giro served warning that the great man's reign as cyclist supreme was well and truly over. When he withdrew from that year's Tour through injury, cycling fans held their breath to see who would assume his crown. The French, of course, had high hopes for reigning champion Bernard Thévenet. But to their horror, it was a couple of Belgians who dominated the race. Sprinter Freddy Maertens wore yellow until the mountains, whereupon the lead passed to Lucien Van Impe, who had won the King of the Mountains title three years in succession. Van Impe duly held onto the *maillot jaune* all the way to Paris. With Thévenet withdrawing through illness, the highest-placed Frenchman was...good old Raymond Poulidor, now aged 40 and appearing in his last Tour, but still good enough to finish third.

TOUR TRIVIA

Feed zones were introduced in 1919, and originally took the form of long trestle tables where riders could stop and load up their jersey pockets with sandwiches and fruit. By the 1950s, however, teams realised that this was an unnecessary waste of valuable time, so instead back-up staff were positioned at set feed zones with cloth bags known as *musettes* full of food. These would be grabbed by the rider on the move, slung over the shoulder, and the food transferred to the jersey before the bag was thrown to the spectators. Today, the feed zones are 545–1,090 yards (500–1,000 m long), and riders face penalties if they receive food outside this area. Team managers are allowed to hand out energy bars and drink bottles from their cars, but not in the first 31 miles (50 km) or the last 12.5 miles (20 km) of a race.

TOUR TRIVIA

Bordeaux is the most-visited Tour town. It has been on the route 76 times in 93 Tours up to and including the 2006 race. The second most-visited is Pau, with 57 appearances.

☆ TOUR STARS WHO DIED IN 1976

Roger Rivière, aged 40: A hugely talented French rider whose career was tragically cut short when he broke his back after crashing into a ravine during the 1960 Tour. (see Cry Me A Rivière)

The vacuum created by the abrupt end of the Eddy Merckx era seemed to have left the Tour in a state of disarray. The 1977 Tour was won for a second time by Bernard Thévenet, but ended in such a cloud of bitterness and recrimination that most people were left wondering why they had bothered. During the race itself, two riders were dismissed after failing dope tests, and as the Tour headed towards Paris, a list of other suspected dopers began to circulate. Top of it was Thévenet himself, who had tested positive in March during the Paris–Nice stage race – but perhaps fearing the repercussions of kicking out the winner of the yellow jersey, and a Frenchman to boot, the Tour organisers issued a statement clearing Thévenet of any wrongdoing. With the heat off, several months later Thévenet admitted taking banned cortisone. With a hypocrisy sadly typical in the sport, he was immediately castigated by the same authorities and peers who knew about and perpetuated the widespread abuse of drugs in cycling.

'Remember that Al Capone was arrested by the Feds on a simple charge of tax evasion and that a thousand eminent citizens were ready to swear that "good old Al" had never killed a soul. It's the same thing here – the incomplete manner in which the drugs tests are administered is an outrageous fraud.'

L'Équipe

TOUR TRIVIA

Dutch rider Gerben Karstens was involved in a high-speed crash during a stage of the 1977 Tour, and to the horror of the TV crews and photographers gathered around him, it looked for all the world as if he had suffered fatal injuries as he lay deathly still on the road. Suddenly, Karstens opened his eyes, burst out laughing and got back on his bike. For his dubious prank, he was roundly admonished by Tour organiser Jacques Goddet.

1977: THE LAST OF MERCKX

Quite why Eddie Merckx decided to compete in the 1977 Tour is something only he can answer. After all, he had nothing to prove. Still, the Cannibal's last hurrah was a typical exhibition of courage and determination in a Tour wracked with suspicion and back-biting. He even won a stage, albeit after the first two riders over the line in St Etienne were disqualified for doping. Unfortunately, any chance he had of reaching the podium was ruined by a debilitating bout of dysentery – although typically this did not stop him reaching Paris.

TOUR TRIVIA

It was perhaps symptomatic of the 1977 Tour that the favourite Lucien Van Impe's race should end after he was knocked into a ditch by a TV car on the Col du Glandon.

TOUR WINNERS BY NATION

36: France
18: Belgium
9: Italy, USA
4: Luxembourg
2: Holland, Switzerland
1: Denmark, Germany, Ireland

☆ TOUR STARS BORN IN 1977

David Millar: A hugely promising Tour rider, who won the yellow jersey after the 2000 Prologue, Millar appeared to have blown his career when he was convicted of doping offences prior to the start of the 2004 Tour. After a two-year ban, the Scot returned in 2006 where he performed creditably in the Tour, later winning a stage in the Vuelta.

ANATOMY OF A LEGEND: BERNARD HINAULT

Hinault was born in the town of Yffiniac in Brittany in 1954. As a boy he was a cross-country champion, and his parents wanted him to work in a bank. A natural cyclist, the young Hinault used to train by racing lorries up a steep hill on the outskirts of the town.

In May 1971, aged sixteen, he entered his first race using a bike borrowed from his brother Gilbert and won with a 434 ft (700 m) sprint from the finish. At the age of seventeen he was crowned French Junior Champion.

Vive le Tour!

In 1977, two years after turning pro, he burst onto the scene by winning the Dauphiné Libéré, Ghent-Wevelgem, GP Nations time trial, Liège–Bastogne–Liège and the Tour of Nations.

His aggressive style earned him the nickname *Blaireau* (Badger) – seemingly because badgers grind their prey's bones to dust after killing them.

He made his Tour debut in 1978, just three weeks after winning the gruelling Vuelta a España and becoming French champion. He won the race by three minutes from Joop Zoetemelk. During the Tour he was accused of being the ringleader of a strike by the riders – something he always denied. However, he soon became known as *Le Patron* thanks to his reputation for bossing the peloton. ('Nobody will attack today because tomorrow is a hard stage' was a typical order.)

Hinault was a hard man. During the 1980 Liège–Bastogne–Liège one-day classic he won despite freezing conditions that forced the abandonment of most of the field. Afterwards, it took three weeks for him to regain feeling in his fingers. In 1985 he completed his record-equalling fifth Tour win despite breaking his nose in a crash.

He had an infamously foul temper, and regularly won the *Prix Citron* awarded by Tour journalists to the sourest rider. He once got his own back by inviting a select few writers to his house to watch a film of one of his victories, only to shock them with a hard-core pornographic movie instead.

Between 1978 and 1986 Hinault appeared in eight Tours, winning five, coming second in two, and failing to finish just one due to a knee injury.

Hinault's last race was a cyclo-cross in November 1986, just four months after completing his final Tour. At his farewell party he was presented with a hook on which to hang his bike. He now works as a cattle breeder and claims never to have ridden a bike since, though he works part-time for the Tour de France organisation committee, helping to plan the route and greet guests, and can often be seen at the side of the podium on stage finishes. In 2002 he called for a life ban for anyone caught using drugs.

1978: TWO STAGE STAGES

Henri Desgrange was famous for manipulating the Tour in any way he could if it meant increasing interest in the event. It was a habit he passed on to his successor Jacques Goddet. While Desgrange liked to invent new mountain routes, Goddet was a firm believer in the two-part stage. Stage one of the 1978 Tour, for example, consisted of an 83 mile (135 km) ride from Leiden to Sint Willebrord in the morning, followed by a 62 mile (100 km) race between Sint Willebrord and Brussels in the afternoon. The riders hated it: it wasn't so much the distances involved, but the sapping logistics that entailed early starts and late finishes, compounded by wearying transfers between finish and start lines. That year, they decided they'd had enough.

On the morning of 12 July, instead of setting out on the first of a two-part stage from Tarbes to Toulouse, stopping off at Valence-d'Agen, the riders dismounted in sight of the finish line and refused to budge until their complaints were acknowledged. The ringleader was alleged to be debutant Bernard Hinault — but although the Badger was photographed in Napoleonic pose at the front of the peloton he always denied he was responsible. Eventually the stage got underway — but the point had been made, and as of the following year the two-part stage was a thing of the past.

Vive le Tour!

'I supported the riders who decided on the spur of the moment to strike at Valence-d'Agen, but to say I was the ringleader is just not true. All the comments made about me and the harsh criticisms that followed affected me deeply.'

Bernard Hinault

'You do not deserve to wear the jersey of the champion of France!'

The Mayor of Valence-d'Agen ticking off Bernard Hinault after being involved with the 1978 riders' strike

1978: POLLENTIER TAKES THE P***

Belgium's Michel Pollentier was regarded as a real Tour favourite in 1978 after winning the previous year's Giro, and seemed to be fulfilling his potential when he assumed the yellow jersey in the mountains. Then came one of the most extraordinary – not to mention pitiful – incidents in Tour history. Summoned to a random drug test, Pollentier was asked to give a urine sample. When he appeared to be having difficulty, the doctor grew suspicious and pulled up his jersey to reveal a rubber bottle of prepared urine and a tube. Both he and Antoine Gutierrez, who was wearing a similar contraption, were immediately disqualified.

1978: BRAVO HINAULT

Bernard Hinault may have made a name for himself at the head of the rider's strike in 1978, but by winning the race he sent a far more ominous message to the cycling world. The win was secured with a sensational time trial on stage twenty which wrested the yellow jersey from Joop Zoetemelk and relegated the Dutchman to yet another second place.

☆ TOUR STARS WHO DIED IN 1978

George Speicher, aged 70: The unexpected French winner of the 1933 Tour, who became World Champion later that same year.

1979: LUCKY ESCAPE FOR FREDDY

Belgian rider Freddy Maertens won three green 'points' jerseys during his fourteen year career, but the biggest break in his life came on 25 May 1979. Suffering from a mystery ailment, Maertens flew to the USA in a bid to get himself in shape for that year's Tour. At New York he disembarked, and the American Airlines DC-10 in which he had flown from Amsterdam continued to Chicago. A few seconds after taking off from Chicago en route to Los Angeles, the DC-10's engine fell off and the plane plummeted into the ground. All 271 passengers were killed.

1979: CHAMP ON THE CHAMPS

Having dominated the flat stages and annihilated the opposition in the Alps, Bernard Hinault arrived in Paris with his second successive Tour win secured. But, typically, this was not good enough for the man who, like Merckx, liked to rub his rivals' noses in it. So it was that Hinault not only entered the Champs Élysées in the *maillot jaune*, but won the sprint finish against his old foe Joop Zoetemelk to finish the Tour in grand style.

1980: THE BALLAD OF THE BADGER'S KNEE

At times it seemed that only a roadside bomb could deflect Bernard Hinault from his *raison d'être* of winning the Tour de France, and even then it would only cost him a few seconds. But in 1980, having won back-to-back Tours, the Badger was scuppered by, of all things, tendonitis in the right knee. Not that this most debilitating of cycling injuries stopped Hinault from reaching the Pyrenees. But as the French public watched with bated breath it became clear that their great hero was struggling, and sure enough after completing stage twelve from Agen to Pau, Hinault's manager Cyril Guimard announced the great man was withdrawing. Hinault, meanwhile, was nowhere to be found. As the race continued, the media switched its attention to playing Hunt the Badger, dispatching reporters throughout France to find him. Eventually Hinault turned up in the pilgrimage destination of Lourdes. If he was seeking a miracle cure for his knee, his performance in the following year's Tour proved that he had found one.

LONGEST POST-WAR BREAKAWAY VICTORIES (since 1947)

157 miles (253 km): Albert Bourlon (1947)
145 miles (234 km): Thierry Marie (1991)
138 miles (223 km): José Perez-Frances (1965)
137 miles (222 km): Bernard Quilfen (1977)
132 miles (214 km): Maurice Blomme (1950)
127 miles (205 km): Pierre Beuffeuil (1966)
124 miles (200 km): Marcel Dussault (1950).

1980: JOOP – AT LAST!

As a teenager, Joop Zoetemelk was a regional speed-skating champion in his native Holland, and there must have been times during his long cycling career when he wondered if he'd have had better luck if he'd stuck to skates instead of pedals. In terms of the Tour de France, the Dutchman would have been within his rights to consider himself cursed; after all, his career just happened to coincide with those of five-times winners Eddy Merckx and Bernard Hinault. Raymond Poulidor may have been dubbed 'The Eternal Second', but he was only runner-up twice: Zoetemelk was second no fewer than six times. When he did finally succeed in winning the race on his ninth attempt in 1980, the feat was largely dismissed because Hinault had been forced to withdraw with a knee injury.

Still, Zoetemelk remains a watchword for consistency and longevity in the sport. It has been calculated that if Tour wins counted for ten points down to one for tenth place, the Dutchman would be the greatest rider in history. Indeed, between 1970 and 1982 he never finished lower than eighth. He spent a total of 22 days in yellow and won ten stages. In

1985, at the venerable age of 38, he became the oldest man to win the World Championship.

All this from a man who in 1973 was given the last rites in hospital after a horrific crash in the Midi-Libre race, then recovered only to find himself at death's door again with a bout of meningitis.

☆ TOUR STARS WHO DIED IN 1980

Lucien Buysse, aged 88: A Belgian rider who competed in eight Tours between 1914 and 1930, winning in 1925 at the age of 32.

André Leducq, aged 76: Leducq won the Tour in 1930 and 1932, and wore the yellow jersey for a total of 25 days – a record that stood for over 40 years until it was beaten by Eddy Merckx.

Gastone Nencini, aged 49: Chain-smoking Nencini won the King of the Mountains title in 1957 and the Tour itself in 1960. The Italian was known as a fearless descender, and was just in front of Roger Rivière on the Col de Perjuret when the Frenchman fell into a ravine while trying to keep up.

Jean Robic, aged 59: A French rider who won the first post-war Tour in 1947.

1981: HATRICK FOR HINAULT

Having withdrawn from the 1980 Tour, Bernard Hinault stated his intentions the following year when he won the opening Prologue time trial by a remarkable 7 seconds – remarkable because the Prologue course was just 3.6 miles (5.9 km) long. Having captured yellow he wore it for nineteen of the 24 stages, winning the race by 14 minutes 34 seconds from Lucien Van Impe – the greatest margin victory since Luis Ocaña in 1973.

TOUR TRIVIA

The first American rider to enter the Tour was Jonathan Boyer in 1981. Boyer was regarded as something as a Californian weirdo by the European cycling community, both for his deeply held religious beliefs and (mainly) for the fact he was a vegetarian. Indeed, he arrived at the start line in Nice with 50 lb (23 kg) of nuts and dates stuffed in the back pockets of his stars and stripes jersey. Boyer finished 32nd in 1981, and in his four subsequent appearances in the Tour his highest placing was twelth in 1983. Still, he was good enough for Eddy Merckx to remark that 'America will be the land of the future of cycling' – not a bad prediction considering Greg Lemond and Lance Armstrong were just around the corner. Sadly for Boyer, his future was a year in jail in 2002 for molesting an underage girl who was part of his church community in California.

'As a rider you know nothing of the race except a blur of faces and that you are the lead actors in a film.'

Charly Mottet, French climber

TOUR TRIVIA

Phil Anderson became the first Australian to wear the *maillot jaune* in 1981.

1982: UP THE WORKERS!

In 1978 it was the riders who went on strike over doping controls. Four years later, the riders found themselves kicking their heels when industrial action first by steel workers in Normandy led to the cancellation of a stage, then farmers in the Alps caused delays by blockading the road.

1982: JUST FOR STARTERS

The 1982 Tour set a new record of 169 starters – 109 more than the first Tour back in 1903. It made little difference to Bernard Hinault whether he had eight or 168 to beat, though. He coasted to his fourth Tour victory ahead of the luckless Joop Zoetemelk yet again, including a second win on the Champs Élysées.

☆ TOUR STARS WHO DIED IN 1982

Victor Fontan, aged 89: A French rider who competed in four Tours between 1924 and 1930, finishing seventh in 1928 – an unremarkable record until one considers that he was shot twice in the leg during World War One. He is also remembered for waking up an entire village in the middle of the night for a replacement bike after his own was broken in a pothole.

TIME-TRIAL BIKE

In a traditional individual time trial, riders set off alone at intervals from one to five minutes, and try to complete the course in as short a time as possible. Although good technique and aerodynamic positioning is vital, bike technology is also important. By using aerodynamic components, such as forward-facing handlebars, disc wheels, and an all-carbon frame and wheels, a time-trial bicycle can be designed to minimize its drag coefficient, allowing a rider to drop their time by minutes over the duration of a long course.

MOST TIME-TRIAL VICTORIES (INCLUDING PROLOGUES)

20: Bernard Hinault
16: Eddy Merckx
11: Jacques Anquetil
10: Miguel Indurain, Lance Armstrong
5: Joop Zoetemelk

Vive le Tour!

1983: VIVA COLOMBIA

In 1983 a team from Colombia made its first appearance in the Tour. The highest finisher was Edgar Corredor, who came in at sixteenth place, 26 minutes behind winner Laurent Fignon.

LIGGETTISMS

For more than 30 years the so-called 'English Voice of the Tour' has been Scouse-born TV commentator Phil Liggett. In that time, Liggett has become something of a cult figure among cycling fans, not least for his habit of lapsing into obscure flights of fancy when describing the action. Here is a selection of some of the best 'Liggettisms'.

'To wear the yellow jersey is to mingle with the gods of cycling.'

'Once again they've stretched the elastic…and now the elastic has snapped!'

'Dancing on the pedals in the polka-dot jersey.'

'Once you pull on that golden fleece you become two men.'

'This is a pedigree group of men – they're hanging on by the skin of their shorts.'

'He's really having to dig deeply into the suitcase of courage.'

1983: VIVE LE PROFESSEUR PONYTAIL

Born in 1960, Fignon was known as *le Professeur* on account of his scholarly appearance (in particular, the wire-rimmed glasses he always wore while racing), the fact he was from Paris, and that he had been to medical school. If this didn't make him stand out enough from the peloton, then his fetching blond ponytail most certainly did – especially as that was all that most of his rivals saw of him in 1983 and 1984 as he romped to two wins out of two attempts.

☆ TOUR STARS WHO DIED IN 1983

Louison Bobet, aged 58: Bobet was the first man to win three Tours in a row (1953, 1954 and 1955), and prior to the arrival of Anquetil was France's greatest rider. His legend was assured when he rode into Paris as victor on the 50th anniversary of the Tour.

Romain Maes, aged 69: A Belgian rider who contested four Tours between 1934 and 1939 and won the race in 1935.

Antonin Magne, aged 79: The legendary French rider who competed in ten Tours between 1927 and 1938, winning in 1931 and 1934 and never finishing lower than eighth.

1984: THE FUTURE IS FIGNON?

When Laurent Fignon won the Tour de France on his debut in 1983, then again in 1984, it seemed the event was about to undergo a seamless transition from one French legend – Bernard Hinault – to another. The first win may have been slightly degraded in the eyes of the purists because his chief rival, Pascal Simon, was forced to quit the race after riding six days with a broken collarbone, while Joop Zoetemelk was kicked out for failing a drugs test; but there was nothing wrong with the second. Up against a fit-again Hinault, the 23-year-old Fignon skinned the four-times Tour champ in the Pyrenees then thrashed him in the last two time trials to win by more than ten minutes in Paris. A star was born, or so it seemed. Few suspected it would be Fignon's last Tour de France win.

'The most remarkable thing about this young man is the robust health he showed at the end of a particularly tough route. His physical freshness is in perfect harmony with his state of mind, his clarity of judgement and his responsible attitude – everything about him displays balance and reason.'

L'Équipe describes Laurent Fignon

TOUR TRIVIA

Robert Millar of Scotland became the first – and so far only – British winner of the King of the Mountains jersey in 1984.

'Those guys see the race on TV then ask you what's happened. You see them sleeping during the day because they've been drunk the night before. If I think they're useless I tell them so.'

Robert Millar vents his spleen at the Tour press pack

☆ TOUR STARS WHO DIED IN 1984

Joaquim Agostinho, aged 42: Born in Portugal, Agostinho was a climber and sprinter who appeared in thirteen Tours between 1969 and 1983, and came third twice. This last podium place was in 1979, at the age of 36. He promised he would race until he was 50, but his life was cut short in 1984 when a dog ran in front of his bike during the Tour of the Algarve. In the resulting crash Agostinho suffered fatal head injuries.

Pierre Brambilla, aged 65: A swiss-born rider who competed in five Tours between 1947 and 1951, finishing third on his debut after having the yellow jersey snatched away from him on the last stage by Jean Robic.

1985: FANTASTIC FIVE

The previous year, after being wiped out in the hills and the time trials by Laurent Fignon, the great Bernard Hinault had been written off as an old has-been. In 1985, he won the Giro d'Italia and suddenly, at the age of 30, the has-been was suddenly red-hot favourite again — especially when Fignon withdrew through injury. *Le Blaireau* did not waste the opportunity, rolling back the years to win the opening prologue time trial, then cementing what would prove to be an unassailable lead by winning stage eight's 60 mile (75 km) time trial by a whopping 2 minutes 20 seconds from Ireland's up-and-coming Stephen Roche. It was not all plain-sailing, however. A spectacular high-speed crash just a few hundred metres from the finish line in St Etienne left Hinault with a broken nose, which hampered him in the mountains and prevented him from extending his lead further. It mattered not: his fifth Tour victory by over 1 minute 40 seconds put Bernard Hinault up among the greats of cycling.

1985: AN INAUSPICIOUS START

The 1985 Tour saw the debut of a 21-year-old Spaniard called Miguel Indurain. The man who would go on to win five Tours de France finished 100th in the Prologue and abandoned on stage four.

☆ TOUR STARS WHO DIED IN 1985

Nicolas Frantz, aged 85: Frantz was the second rider from Luxembourg to win the Tour, in 1927. He competed in seven Tours between 1924 and 1932.

TOUR WINNERS 1969–1985

1969: Eddy Merckx (BEL), [KoM: Eddy Merckx; Points: Eddy Merckx]

1970: Eddy Merckx (BEL), [KoM: Eddy Merckx; Points: Walter Godefroot (BEL)]

1971: Eddy Merckx (BEL), [KoM: Lucien Van Impe (BEL); Points: Eddy Merckx]

1972: Eddy Merckx (BEL), [KoM: Lucien Van Impe (BEL); Points: Eddy Merckx]

1973: Luis Ocaña (SPA), [KoM: Pedro Torres (SPA); Points: Herman van Springel (BEL)]

1974: Eddy Merckx (BEL), [KoM: Domingo Perurena (SPA); Points: Patrick Sercu (BEL)]

1975: Bernard Thévenet (FRA), [KoM: Lucien Van Impe (BEL); Points: Rik van Linden (BEL)]

1976: Lucien Van Impe (BEL): [KoM: Giancarlo Bellini (ITA); Points: Freddy Maertens (BEL)]

1977: Bernard Thévenet (FRA): [KoM: Lucien Van Impe (BEL); Points: Jacques Esclassan (FRA)]

Vive le Tour!

1978: Bernard Hinault (FRA), [KoM: Mariano Martinez (FRA); Points: Freddy Maertens (BEL)]

1979: Bernard Hinault (FRA), [KoM: Giovanni Battaglin (ITA); Points: Bernard Hinault]

1980: Joop Zoetemelk (NED), [KoM: Raymond Martin (FRA); Points: Rudy Pevenage (BEL)]

1981: Bernard Hinault (FRA), [KoM: Lucien Van Impe (BEL); Points: Freddy Maertens (BEL)]

1982: Bernard Hinault (FRA), [KoM: Bernard Vallet (FRA); Points: Sean Kelly (IRE)]

1983: Laurent Fignon (FRA), [KoM: Lucien Van Impe (BEL); Points: Sean Kelly (IRE)]

1984: Laurent Fignon (FRA), [KoM: Robert Millar (SCO); Points: Frank Hoste (BEL)]

1985: Bernard Hinault (FRA), [KoM: Luis Herrera (COL); Points: Sean Kelly (IRE)]

BIG MIG AND THE STAR-SPANGLED BANNER 1986–1998

ANATOMY OF A LEGEND: GREG LEMOND

Born in Lakewood, California, Greg Lemond was among the first US riders to make an impact on the Tour, and as such paved the way for the likes of Lance Armstrong 20 years later. He saw his first bike race from the back of his dad's car as they travelled across the Sierra mountains. He said later that it was 'cool' how his dad couldn't keep up with the riders as they plummeted down the descents.

Until his late teens, Lemond's preferred sport was skiing. He only cycled to keep fit for the winter downhill season. Road racing was virtually unheard of as a sport in the US.

The switch proved inspirational, for Lemond was a natural on two wheels. As an amateur he was World Junior Champion, and in 1983 became America's first World Champion. In 1984 he rode his first Tour and came third. The following year he felt he could have won had he not been on the same team as Bernard Hinault, or indeed had Hinault not been going for his fifth Tour win.

A gruelling duel with Hinault followed in 1986, after which Lemond became the USA's first winner of the Tour de France. A glittering period of domination beckoned – but the following spring, disaster struck. While out hunting in the woods, Lemond was accidentally shot by his brother-in-law. Over 40 shotgun pellets ripped through his body, lodging not only in his back and legs, but more critically in his small intestine, liver, diaphragm, and the lining of his heart. While waiting for rescue, his right lung collapsed and he lost three quarters of his blood supply. Had it not been for a helicopter ambulance in the vicinity, it is probable that Lemond would have bled to death. In the event, his life was only just saved by emergency surgery – and to this day he still has shotgun pellets lodged in his body.

Lemond's Tour comeback in 1988 was disastrous, and there were many who thought he should quit the sport. In truth, he should never have competed, having lost over 20 lb (9 kg) of muscle mass after the shooting.

In 1989 Lemond won a titanic battle with Laurent Fignon when he turned a 50-second deficit into an 8 second win in the last time trial on the last day of the Tour. Lemond won again in 1990, but it would be his last Tour success. He retired from the sport in 1994 after failing to complete the race. Today, Lemond runs his own bike manufacturing company, but suffers from the wasting disease muscular myopathy, which has been attributed to the effects of the shooting.

1986: A PROMISE TO GREG . . . SORT OF

In theory there was nothing to stop Bernard Hinault winning a sixth Tour in 1986 – except for the fact that the previous year he had promised payback to his young American team-mate Greg Lemond who had selflessly reined in his own ambitions to help the injured Badger win the race. 'In '86 the Tour will be for you,' Hinault told Lemond. 'I will be there to help you.'

As the race progressed, however, Lemond could have been forgiven for thinking that with allies like Hinault, he did not need enemies. No sooner did the peloton reach the Pyrenees than the old man raced away and opened a 4 minute lead on the American. The following day Lemond clawed back the time, but the rest of the race was ridden under a cloud of mutual suspicion. When Lemond finally opened a gap on Hinault on stage seventeen, he thought that was surely that – but the following day Hinault was at it again. This time the Frenchman launched an audacious attack on the descent of the Galibier, and had it not been for the efforts of Canadian Steve Bauer, Lemond might not have been able to catch him. As the two riders reached the finish line at Alpe d'Huez together it was all smiles and congratulations, although Lemond must have felt like belting Hinault for all the grief he had caused. Lemond was in yellow, the first American to win the Tour. Even then Hinault wasn't finished, winning the final time trial by 25 seconds in order to re-emphasise that the king did not give up his crown so easily.

☆ TOUR STARS WHO DIED IN 1986

Alfredo Binda, aged 84: A brilliant cyclist in the 1920s and 1930s, and one of the first true professionals of the sport, in 1930 Binda earned the rare accolade of being paid by the Giro organisers *not* to compete in the race he had won four times, while being paid by Henri Desgrange to make his debut in the Tour de France. It was his only appearance, but later he expertly managed the Italian team containing the opposing personalities and talents of Fausto Coppi and Gino Bartali.

Vive le Tour!

Vincent Trueba, aged 81: Trueba was the first King of the Mountains in 1933; and was known by the nickname 'The Flea of Torrelavega'.

1987: ANYBODY'S JERSEY

With Greg Lemond recovering from a near-fatal shooting accident, Bernard Hinault retired, and Laurent Fignon in lousy form, the *maillot jaune* in the 1987 Tour was generally thought to be anybody's. And so it proved. In all a then record eight different riders wore yellow: Jelle Nijdam of Holland, Poland's Lech Piasecki (the first Eastern European to lead the Tour), Erich Maechler of Switzerland, Charlie Mottet, Martial Gayant and Jean-François Bernard of France, Pedro Delgado of Spain and Stephen Roche of Ireland.

TOUR TRIVIA
The 1987 Tour Prologue was held in the divided city of Berlin for the first time.

1987: THE UNSTOPPABLE IRISH

Ireland consistently supplied top quality riders to the Tour. Shay Elliot became the first Irishman to wear yellow in 1963 (see Green and Yellow. page 108), while the great Sean Kelly won the green jersey of points winner in 1982, 1983, 1985 and 1989. In 1987, however, the Emerald Isle had its greatest-ever year when Stephen Roche snatched the yellow jersey on the penultimate stage time trial and held onto it into Paris by just 40 seconds from Pedro Delgado. Mind you, he had already won the

Giro that year. Later he would go on to become World Champion – a treble feat which only Eddy Merckx had ever achieved.

1987: ROCHE v DELGADO

The battle between Stephen Roche and Pedro Delgado in the Alps has gone down in Tour legend. Having dislodged the Irishman from the lead on stage twenty to Alpe d'Huez, Delgado looked to deliver the *coup de grâce* the following day on the gruelling stage to the mountain-top finish at La Plagne. And it seemed he had done enough when, after following the break by Laurent Fignon, Delgado raced away from the obviously struggling Roche. The seconds ticked by, and with them it seemed any chance of Roche winning the Tour – but then, materialising like a spectre out of the fog, the Irishman appeared at the summit. Delgado could not believe it, and neither could anyone else. Riding to the very peak of his endurance, Roche had somehow managed one last, lung-bursting effort to keep him within 40 seconds – touching distance of the Spaniard. Although he was so exhausted he had to be given oxygen, Roche had recovered sufficiently the next day to reduce the lead even further to just 21 seconds. Second place in the time trial gave him a lead of 40 seconds, and the first-ever Irish success in the Tour de France.

ALL HAIL ROCHE

On his return to Ireland after winning the Giro, the Tour and the World Championship, Stephen Roche was given a tickertape reception and the freedom of the city of Dublin. His success in 1987 was particularly satisfying to the folk of Dundrum, his home village, who had saved up to buy him his first bike and who had clubbed together to send him to Europe when he was working as a welder in a local dairy factory.

☆ TOUR STARS WHO DIED IN 1987

Jacques Anquetil, aged 53: Four months after the Tour, on 18 November 1987, Jacques Anquetil died at his home near Rouen. The five-times Tour winner had been suffering from stomach cancer. Legend has it that when his great friend and rival Raymond Poulidor went to visit him on his deathbed, Anquetil smiled up at him and said, 'So, Raymond – it looks like you are going to come second again!' Eight thousand people packed into Rouen cathedral for a memorial service to cycling's first great superstar. Anquetil was buried in the town of Quincampoix where, ten years later, former five-time champions Eddy Merckx, Bernard Hinault and Miguel Indurain gathered to pay their respects at a monument erected to display his achievements.

THE HALL OF FAME (NUMBER OF TOUR WINS)

7: Lance Armstrong (USA)
5: Jacques Anquetil (FRA), Eddy Merckx (BEL), Bernard Hinault (FRA), Miguel Indurain (SPA)
3: Philippe Thys (BEL), Louison Bobet (FRA), Greg Lemond (USA)
2: Lucien Petit-Breton (FRA), Firmin Lambot (BEL), Ottavio Bottecchia (ITA), Nicolas Frantz (LUX), Antonin Magne (FRA), Lucien Leducq (FRA), Sylvère Maes (BEL), Gino Bartali (ITA), Fausto Coppi (ITA), Bernard Thévenet (FRA), Laurent Fignon (FRA)

1988: A NEW BROOM

In 1988 the septuagenarian Jacques Goddet handed over the reins of Tour organiser to Jean-Marie Leblanc, the chief cycling correspondent of *L'Équipe*, continuing the tradition that the boss of the Tour is a former journalist. Neither as bombastic as Henri Desgrange, nor as outgoing as Goddet, Leblanc unobtrusively but effectively dragged the Tour towards the 21st century by hacking away at the deadwood that had accumulated over the previous 85 years and raising the profile of the race through major sponsorship and TV deals.

1988: DODGY DELGADO

When is a Tour win not a Tour win? When the winner has tested positive for drugs, perhaps (see: What A Dope, page 250) You would think so – but unfortunately the Tour has a history of massaging the facts so as to prevent undue scandal. Take the case of Pedro Delgado, who in 1988 won the Tour by seven minutes from Holland's Steven Rooks with a victory that many felt could signal the beginning of the next cycling dynasty. Except that on stage nineteen of the race, a routine dope test found traces of probenecid in his system. The drug is not a performance enhancer as such, but it was included on the International Olympic Committee's (IOC) list of banned substances because it can mask the presence of steroids. The shock news swept around the Tour circus, even before the routine second test confirmed the results of the first. Surely the Tour organisers had no option but to boot Delgado out of the race? At the very least they should dock his time. After all, Dutchman

Vive le Tour!

Gert-Jan Theunisse had been docked ten minutes after being found guilty of doping, a decision that effectively put him out of the reckoning of a podium place.

It was then that the lawyers got on their bikes. As the race headed for Paris under a cloud of suspicion and uncertainty, Delgado's legal team discovered that the IOC's ruling on probenecid had not yet been ratified by cycling's governing body, the UCI. The UCI, reluctantly, ruled that the Spaniard had no case to answer.

The case left a sour taste in the mouth, however. Disgusted with Delgado's acquittal and the perceived laxity of Theunisse's time penalty, the riders went on strike before the start of the next stage. Two days later, Pedro Delgado rode up the Champs Élysées waving a huge Spanish flag, the heir apparent to Bahamontés and Ocaña, but a tainted champion in the eyes of the rest of the cycling world.

TOUR TRIVIA

For winning the 1988 Tour, Pedro Delgado got a Peugeot 405 car, an apartment, a piece of art, and the equivalent of £50,000 from the sponsors Crédit Lyonnais.

1989: MISSED THE BOAT

After his dodgy Tour victory in 1988, the following year Pedro Delgado arrived at the Prologue start line in Luxembourg determined to win in style. Unfortunately, he also turned up 2 minutes 40 seconds late, allegedly after signing autographs for his adoring fans. Remarkably, the Spaniard finished the time trial just fourteen seconds behind the winner, Eric Breukink, but nearly three minutes down on the general classification

– almost exactly the difference between himself and the eventual Tour winner Greg Lemond in Paris.

'Even today I can't explain what happened. I wanted to shine from the first pedal. I went to warm up, which I never usually did. I wanted to get away from the Press who hassled me all the time and I also wanted to keep my concentration. It was this and nothing else that made me late. None of the Press meditations about my late start were true. I called myself stupid. The worst repercussion wasn't so much the time lost so stupidly, but that I couldn't forgive myself and lost a night's sleep over my own anger.'

Pedro Delgado attempts to explain why he missed his start time

TOP TEN HIGHEST TOUR CLIMBS

Name	Altitude	Location	First climbed
Col de Restefond	9,193 ft (2,802 m)	Alps	1962
Col d'Iseran	9,068 ft (2,764 m)	Alps	1938
Col du Galibier	8,681 ft (2,646 m)	Alps	1911
Col du Grand St Bernard	8,100 ft (2,469 m)	Alps	1949
Col du Granon	7,917 ft (2,413 m)	Alps	1986
Port d'Envalira	7,900 ft (2,408 m)	Pyrenees	1964
Col d'Izoard	7,743 ft (2,360 m)	Alps	1922
Col de la Cayolle	7,631 ft (2,326 m)	Alps	1950
Val Thorens	7,464 ft (2,275 m)	Alps	1994
Col d'Allos	7,372 ft (2,247 m)	Alps	1911

Vive le Tour!

☆ TOUR STARS WHO DIED IN 1988

René Vietto, aged 73: Vietto never won any of the eight Tours he attempted, but it certainly wasn't for the want of trying. In 1934, on his debut, he almost certainly would have won had he not been ordered to help his team leader Antonin Magne. Between 1935 and 1939 he was wiped out by crashes and injury and then came six years of war. Remarkably, in 1947, aged 33, he was just three days from victory in Paris when he was annihilated in the final time trial, losing fifteen minutes. That same year, suffering from a sore foot, he ordered the team doctor to cut off his toe. He then ordered him to perform the same operation on young team-mate Apo Lazarides. What makes the story even more bizarre is that Lazarides agreed to the surgery (see Toe the Line, page 67).

1989: EIGHT SECONDS

Rarely has the result of a Tour de France gone to the wire as it did in 1989. The chances of it ever happening again are remote. The bare facts show that Greg Lemond won the race from Laurent Fignon by just eight seconds — but this reveals nothing of the gut-wrenching drama of the final time trial to Paris on Sunday 23 July. By then, cycling fans had already been treated to an extraordinary duel between two former winners making their very different comebacks in the Tour: Lemond, after the shooting accident of 1987, and Fignon, after what looked like a career-threatening loss of form. For nine stages between Rennes and Gap, no more than seven seconds had separated the two men, as first the American and then the Frenchman grasped the *maillot jaune*. In the Alps it was a different story, and by the time they reached Paris, Fignon was fully 50 seconds ahead of Lemond. What lay ahead was a 15.2 mile (24.5 km) time trial from Versailles to Paris; not even the wildest American optimist could imagine Fignon could blow a lead of nearly a minute over such a distance.

Fignon couldn't either – which is possibly the only explanation for what happened next. Today, Lemond's bulbous aero helmet and handlebars look impossibly archaic. But at the time they were regarded as state-of-the-art equipment. Fignon, by contrast, turned up to the start gate in his wire-rimmed specs and sporting a familiar ponytail. It swiftly became obvious that neither were as aerodynamic as Lemond's gear. By the halfway stage, Lemond had chewed a massive bite out of Fignon's 50 second lead. By the time a shattered Fignon crossed the line on the Champs Élysées, the 50 second lead had turned into an eight second deficit. As Lemond whooped with joy, Fignon collapsed in tears into the arms of his disbelieving back-up team. It was the closest finish in Tour history, by far the most dramatic, and a shattering blow to French pride. Lemond was back, and the Americans were once again a force to be reckoned with in world cycling.

1989: LEMOND v FIGNON – THE DUEL IN THE SUN

The ding-dong battle between Greg Lemond and Laurent Fignon in 1989 was reminiscent of a boxing match.

ROUND ONE: All-square as Fignon and Lemond finish the Prologue in Luxembourg with the same time.

ROUND TWO: *Bash!* Fignon sends Lemond reeling with a 51-second advantage after the team time trial, again in Luxembourg.

169

Vive le Tour!

ROUND THREE: *Cra-aak!* Back comes Lemond at the individual time trial between Dinard and Rennes, grabbing the yellow jersey by just five seconds.

ROUND FOUR: *Smash!* Fignon storms to the summit finish at Superbagnères seven seconds ahead of Lemond and wearing yellow.

ROUND FIVE: *Ooo-oof!* Ace time-trialler Lemond grabs the yellow by 40 seconds after the 39 km sprint from Gap to Orcières-Merlette.

ROUND SIX: *Bosh!* Fignon is on the ropes as Lemond increases his lead to 53 seconds on stage sixteen.

ROUND SEVEN: *Boof!* Fignon storms back at Alpe d'Huez, leaving Lemond for dead and regaining the lead by 26 seconds.

ROUND EIGHT: *Clang!* Just three stages to go, and Fignon extends his lead to 50 seconds. Lemond is reeling now. Surely the end is nigh.

ROUND NINE: *Sma-aack!* The final day, the final time trial and Lemond decks Fignon with the decisive sucker punch, winning the Tour by eight seconds and leaving the Frenchman out for the count.

'Lemond is trying not to smile. Millions of pairs of eyes hang on the luminous digits: forty-eight, forty-nine… A collective gasp roars over the bitumen. On the greatest avenue in the world the blue-eyed American has signed one of the most beautiful exploits in Tour history.'

L'Équipe waxes lyrical about Greg Lemond's win in 1989

TOUR TRIVIA

Raúl Alcalá's win in the stage from Luxembourg to Francorchamps was the first by a Mexican rider.

☆ TOUR STARS WHO DIED IN 1989

Charles Holland, aged 81: Birmingham-born Holland made history in 1937 when he and fellow countryman Bill Burl became the first British riders to start the Tour. Unfortunately, neither man finished (see Holland – The Pride of Britain, page 59).

1990: THE START OF SOMETHING LONG-LASTING

In 1990 the Tour organisers broke with tradition when they invited a professional team from the Soviet Union to take part in the race for the first time. Drilled in the training schools of Russia and East Germany, the team made an immediate impact: Dmitri Konchyev wore the polka-dot jersey of King of the Mountains for four stages, then won stage eighteen from Lourdes to Pau, while Olaf Ludwig, an East German, won a stage and the points competition. An early holder of the white jersey for best young rider was Viatcheslav Ekimov, a callow 24-year old from Leningrad. It's doubtful even he could have suspected that he would be riding his final Tour sixteen years later, at the age of 40 and the oldest rider in the peloton.

1990: ALMOST A BREAK TOO FAR

The 1990 Tour was almost over before it started. On stage one the peloton huffed and puffed while a breakaway of four riders scarpered unmolested up the road and secured a lead of more than ten minutes. These were no flash-in-the-pan riders, either. They included Steve Bauer of Canada, who had finished fourth overall two years earlier, Ronan Pensec, who had come sixth and seventh in 1986 and 1988, and the exciting young Italian Claudio Chiappucci, who had won the King of the Mountains title in that year's Giro d'Italia. When these three men went on to share the yellow jersey all the way through the Alps and Pyrenees, to within two stages of Paris, the extent of the peloton's error was abundantly clear (see The Peloton Plays Dumb, page 248).

Fortunately, at least one of the bunch was on the ball – two-times winner Greg Lemond had assiduously chipped away at the lead so that by the time the race reached the penultimate stage, a short time trial around Lac de Vassivière, he was just five seconds behind the *maillot jaune* Chiappucci. That, effectively, made it game, set and match to the American time trial specialist, who duly took the lead into Paris with a cushion of over two minutes.

☆ TOUR STARS WHO DIED IN 1990

Max Bulla, aged 85: In 1931 Bulla became the first Austrian rider to wear the *maillot jaune*, and he did so as an independent amateur, or *touriste-routier*, winning a stage from Caen to Dinan against the odds.

ANATOMY OF A LEGEND: MIGUEL INDURAIN

Miguel Indurain, only the fourth man to achieve five Tour de France victories and the first to win them in successive years (1991–1995), was born in Villava, Spain, on 16 July 1964. He won his first race at the age of eleven, and at the age of fourteen had successfully applied for a racing licence.

Indurain was designed to be a cyclist. Tall and muscular, he was a devastating time-triallist but could also hold his own in the mountains thanks to a resting heart-rate of just 29 bpm and a lung capacity of an astonishing eight litres. The Belgian rider Johan Bruyneel once described riding behind Indurain as 'like taking pace from a motorbike.'

His Tour nicknames were variously Big Mig, or The Terminator, but in truth Indurain was such an obdurately uninteresting character that journalists would try anything to make him sound more interesting.

Although he would end up as one of the legends of the sport, Indurain's initial forays into the Tour de France were less than startling: his first two attempts in 1985 and 1986 ended with abandons, while in 1987 he finished an ignominious 97th.

A virtual unknown, Indurain was finally noticed by the public in 1990 when he came from nowhere to win a tough mountain stage to the summit of Luz-Ardiden. That year he would finish tenth.

Indurain became the fourth Spaniard after Federico Bahamontés, Luis Ocaña and Pedro Delgado to win the Tour de France. In 1988, he had been Delgado's *domestique*.

In 1999 Indurain was voted Spain's athlete of the century. He wore the Tour's yellow jersey for a total of 59 days.

British yellow jersey holder Chris Boardman summed up Indurain when he said: 'Indurain makes me sick because he's actually a really nice guy. You can't actually work yourself up, there's no hate involved, no anger. He's a really nice bloke and a true champion.'

TOUR TRIVIA
Mauro Ribeiro became the first Brazilian cyclist to win a Tour stage in 1991 when he led the field to victory in Rennes.

1991: THE KING IS DEAD, LONG LIVE THE KING

In 1991 Greg Lemond went in search of his fourth Tour victory, but despite wearing yellow for five days in total, the American never looked as confident as in previous years. Indeed, the writing was arguably on the wall after the first individual time trial on stage eight when he was beaten into second place by eight seconds by Miguel Indurain. A few days later in the Pyrenees, Lemond was visibly suffering as the race leaders crossed the summit of the Tourmalet seventeen seconds ahead of him. By the end of the stage, Indurain was in yellow and would remain in it all the way to Paris.

1991: A STRANGE CASE OF FOOD POISONING

Following the Tour's arrival in the town of Quimper at the end of stage ten, the entire PDM team – including Irish rider Martin Earley – withdrew as one from the race. The official line was that the team was suffering from food poisoning, although it was rumoured that the sickness bout was actually caused by an adverse reaction to doping products.

TOUR TRIVIA

Ralph Sorensen of Denmark was the proud wearer of the yellow jersey for four stages until he crashed into a traffic island and was forced to retire injured.

1991: OUCH-OV!

There was another great performance by the newly admitted Soviet riders in 1991, especially from Djamolidine Abdoujaparov who won the points jersey. Not that it was a painless victory for Abdoujaparov. Racing at top speed in a bunch sprint up the Champs Élysées, he touched wheels and smashed head-first into a roadside advertising hoarding with just a few hundred metres to go. His bike destroyed, Abdoujaparov crossed the line on foot several minutes later – but kept the jersey because Tour rules state that riders who crash in the final kilometre record the same finishing time as the rest of the bunch.

TOUR TRIVIA

The team of construction and logistics workers responsible for ensuring the start and finish areas, and the riders', journalists' and sponsors' compounds, are built – as well as repairing worn tarmac on the stage route – are known as the Orange Brigade because of their bright orange overalls.

1991: ABDOUJAPAROV USM

Djamolidine Abdoujaparov had a reputation for being a real nutter on the bike, and many of his bunch sprint victories were arguably the result of other riders keeping their distance as the so-called Tashkent Terror hurtled towards the line. His career was sparkling – three green 'points' jerseys in the mid-1990s – but it was also brief. In 1997, aged 33, he retired in the face of a two-year ban for doping offences. The following year, rock musician and cycling fan Les Carter, formerly of Carter USM, formed a new band called Abdoujaparov in honour of his hero.

1992: UNSTOPPABLE INDURAIN

What had looked an ominous foretaste of things to come in 1991 proved accurate the following year when Miguel Indurain won his second Tour by effectively putting his foot on its throat and pressing down until its resistance was gone. The Spaniard came into the race having already won the Giro d'Italia three weeks earlier by dint of his superlative time-trialling ability allied with a stubbornness in the mountains. Within a few minutes of the Tour commencing, it was clear nothing had changed. In San Sebastian, in front of a huge and adoring Basque crowd, Indurain swept to yellow in the 8 km Prologue.

Although he lost it the following day, everyone knew that it was only a case of waiting until the next time trial until he won it back again. Sure enough, in the 41 mile (65 km) circuit around Luxembourg, Indurain destroyed the field – in a highly symbolic moment, he overtook former Tour champion Laurent Fignon, who had set off six minutes ahead of him. A couple of days later, in the Alps, Indurain snatched back the *maillot jaune* and kept it all the way to Paris, pausing only to win his third time trial of the race along the way, covering the 40 miles (64 km) at a staggering average speed of 32.51 mph (52.349 kph).

1992: THE LONG ROAD TO SESTRIERE

Solo breakaways rarely succeed. Most of the time they are the cycling equivalent of fifteen minutes of fame, a chance for an unknown rider to give himself and his shirt sponsor a rare taste of TV airtime for an hour or two before he is gobbled up by the relentless pack. When a rider *does* manage to stay ahead, though, it provides one of the magical moments of the sport. And in 1992, Italy's Claudio Chiappucci did just that on the long and tortuous Alpine stage from St-Gervais, at the foot of Mont Blanc, to the ski station at Sestriere 157 miles (254 km) away. Perhaps anxious to cement himself as a legitimate Tour contender after finishing second and third in his first two Tours, or perhaps spurred on by the thousands of Italian fans lining the route towards the Italian border, Chiappucci broke away with a small group of riders after just 30 miles (50 km), then set off on his own with 78 miles (125 km) to go.

With several mountains to cross before Sestriere, few thought the Italian would survive in the sapping heat. Yet on he went, relentlessly turning the pedals and getting further and further from the peloton. Suddenly, Indurain and the other leaders realised that Chiappucci's daring solo assault could well secure him the yellow jersey and set off in hot pursuit. Chiappucci, however, was not to be caught that day. His arrival at Sestriere was greeted by a sea of Italian flags and a hero's welcome. In any other year the breakaway would have been good enough to win the Tour – but Indurain was less than two minutes behind, protecting his yellow jersey.

Vive le Tour!

1992: A WORD IN YOUR SHELL-LIKE

The US-based Motorola team caused more than a few raised eyebrows when team leader Phil Anderson arrived at the start line wearing an earpiece. It turned out that the earpiece was connected to a receiver in Anderson's shirt, which in turn was connected remotely to a transmitter fitted underneath the Australian's saddle. The equipment was designed to enable Anderson to receive radio instructions from team manager Jim Ochowicz and had a range of one kilometre. 'It's simply standard Motorola equipment,' said a team spokesman, which rather understated the huge impact the innovation would have on the sport of professional road racing. Before, if a team manager wanted to get information to his riders, he would have to catch up to one of them in the team car. Now all he had to do was speak into a radio fitted onto his dashboard. Soon earpieces were standard within the peloton, much to the disgust of veterans like Bernard Hinault who declared that riders who wore them were 'no more than simply pedalling machines' with little or no appreciation of tactics.

TOUR TRIVIA
In 1992, Basque separatists set fire to a number of cars belonging to journalists following the Tour. One happened to belong to Channel 4's commentator Phil Liggett.

TOUR TRIVIA
The 1992 Tour was the most cosmopolitan ever, visiting six countries en route to Paris. These were: Spain, Belgium, Holland, Germany, Luxembourg and Italy.

'When I started seeing riders with fat arses climbing like aeroplanes, I understood. I preferred to stop.'

Luis Herrera, a Colombian climber, explaining why drug-taking in the peloton became too much for him in 1992

☆ TOUR STARS WHO DIED IN 1992

Jean Aerts, aged 85: A Belgian rider who won eleven stages between 1932 and 1935 and wore the yellow jersey in 1933. He was also the first man to win both the amateur and professional road championship.

1993: INDURAIN AGAIN

Another year, another Giro–Tour double for Miguel Indurain who in 1993 was as imperious in victory as he had been in 1991 and 1992. Once again the foundations of victory were set as early as the 4.2 mile (6.8 km) race Prologue which the Spaniard won by eight seconds from his nearest rival. Once again his lead was reinforced by a crushing victory in the long time trial. The only surprise was that Switzerland's Tony Rominger won the final time trial – but by then Indurain was so far ahead of the field that it made no difference.

1993: THE DEVIL TAKE THE HINDMOST

As he rode towards the stage finish in Andorra, Claudio Chiappucci was somewhat perturbed to discover that he was being followed by a large man dressed in a red devil costume, waving a cardboard pitchfork. This was the first sighting of The Devil, alias German Didi Senff, who has been a regular fixture by the roadside of every Tour since. While he was first regarded with good humour, in recent years his looming presence and bellowed encouragement has served only to annoy the riders, who take great delight in throwing empty water bottles at him. Indeed, today The Devil paints the road with red pitchforks to give the riders time to get their missiles ready.

1993: DEAR PRUDENCIO

Miguel Indurain cruised to victory in the first long time trial of the 1993 Tour, winning by 2 minutes 11 seconds from his nearest rival Gianni Bugno, despite a puncture that cost him a few seconds en route. Trailing in last that day was Prudencio Indurain, Big Mig's younger brother. In fact, were it not for Miguel's puncture holding him up, Prudencio would have finished outside the time limit and been expelled from the race. Brotherly love, indeed.

TOUR TRIVIA

Prudencio Indurain looked so similar to his brother, he would often sign autographs for unwitting fans at race starts, pretending he was Miguel.

1993: FIRST SIGHT OF FUTURE CHAMP

Stage eight was won by a relative unknown from Texas who would later abandon the race. His name? Lance Armstrong.

'I came to learn and to win a stage. I've already learned a lot and I've won a stage. Now I'll carry on learning so I can win again.'

Lance Armstrong after his 1993 Tour debut

LEGENDARY MOUNTAINS OF THE TOUR: IZOARD

A real Tour legend, the 7,746 ft (2,361 m) Izoard in the Alps has witnessed some classic Tour moments since Belgian Philippe Thys first rode over it in 1922. The greatest, and perhaps most poignant, was undoubtedly in 1949 when the young pretender Fausto Coppi caught Tour king Gino Bartali and announced to the world that the old man's reign was over. 'It's my birthday,' Bartali is said to have shouted. 'Let's finish together. Tomorrow you'll win the Tour.' It is also the place where, in 1960, the first televised motorbike pictures were broadcast.

1993: POLE POSITION

Despite the promise of the influx of Soviet riders, Polish cyclist Zenon Jaskula's third place on the podium beside Tony Rominger and Miguel Indurain in Paris made him the first Eastern European to finish in the top-three of the Tour de France.

MOST STAGE WINS BY NATION

652: France
449: Belgium
244: Italy
151: Netherlands
98: Spain
53: Luxembourg
52: Germany
51: Switzerland
31: United States
23: Great Britain
13: Australia, Denmark
12: Columbia
10: Ireland

1994: A SPECTACULAR START

As Tour debuts go, Chris Boardman's in 1994 will take some beating. The 26-year-old from Hoylake, Merseyside, had come to prominence two years earlier when he won Gold for Great Britain in the 4,000 m pursuit at the

Barcelona Olympics. His early career as a professional roadman in Europe had pretty much sunk without a trace, however, until late in 1993 when his time-trialling prowess won him stages at the prestigious Dauphiné Libéré and the Tour of Switzerland. At the following year's Tour, riding for the GAN team, Boardman stunned everyone by winning the 4.4 mile (7.2 km) Prologue in Lille at an average speed of 34.27 mph (55.152 kph), a new Tour record. Most surprised of all was Miguel Indurain, who found himself soundly thrashed by fifteen seconds by the newcomer. Boardman went on to wear yellow for three days, still the best-ever performance by a British rider alongside Scotland's David Millar in 2000.

1994: TUNNEL VISION

The 1994 Tour returned to Britain for the first time in 20 years, to commemorate the 50th anniversary of the D-Day landings. In 1974 the visit had consisted of a single stage up and down the Plympton bypass. This time it was rather more interesting, with the bikes and support vehicles crossing the Channel via the newly opened Eurotunnel, and two days of racing on the south coast. Francisco Cabello won the stage from Dover to Brighton, and Nicola Minali took the following day's stage to Portsmouth. Britain, of course, was already basking in the glory of its very own yellow jersey hero in Chris Boardman. Indeed, this would be a good Tour for the British. The day after the race returned to France, Englishman Sean Yates snatched the *maillot jaune* for the first time in his career, wearing it with pride for a single stage between Rennes and Futuroscope.

1994: GENDARME! CAMERA! CARNAGE!

Bunch sprints – where as many as 50 leaders race helter-skelter for the finish line at speeds in excess of 43 mph (70 kph) – rate only slightly behind high-speed mountain descents for danger. The Tour is littered with instances where the slightest touch of wheels in the final few metres has resulted in a catastrophic collision of men and machines. One of the most spectacular crashes came at the end of the very first stage of the 1994 race, and for once had nothing to do with rider error. With the bunch accelerating towards the line at Armentières, a blue-shirted *gendarme* with a camera stepped out to take a shot of the riders. A split-second later he was hit by sprinters Wilfried Nielsen and Laurent Jalabert. The resulting collision left bodies and mangled bicycles scattered across the tarmac – but astonishingly no one, not even the *gendarme*, was killed. The main casualty was the unfortunate Jalabert, who took the full force of an advertising hoarding against his helmet. Shaken and with blood pouring from a head wound, he somehow managed to stagger across the finish line – but would later withdraw from the race.

TOUR TRIVIA

Crowds of up to 300,000 spectators line the route of the Alpe d'Huez, and it is estimated that one in three of them are Dutch: ever since the first stage was ridden there, the Dutch have made the mountain their own.

1994: INDURAIN… ER, AGAIN

Indurain had been soundly defeated at the Giro. He was desperately lacking form. Surely it was the end for Big Mig. Surely he couldn't make it four in a row?

For the naysayers and French fans alike, 1994 promised to be a good year – especially when Chris Boardman took fifteen seconds off the Spaniard in the opening Prologue at Lille. With young bucks like Laurent Jalabert, Richard Virenque and Luc Leblanc straining at the leash, there was hope in the air of a home win for the first time in nearly a decade.

But Indurain would prove as single-minded about crushing hopes as he was crushing opponents. After the hiccup of losing the Prologue, the Spaniard reasserted his authority with a devastating performance in the 40 mile (64 km) time trial between Périgeux and Bergerac, not only winning it by more than two minutes, but putting fully five minutes between himself and the English upstart Boardman. Point made, and apart from Virenque's victory in the King of the Mountains competition, nobody dared challenge Big Mig again, and he cruised home for his fourth successive Tour win.

☆ TOUR STARS WHO DIED IN 1994

Luis Ocaña, aged 48: The Spaniard who gave Eddy Merckx a run for his money, Ocaña won one Tour in 1973 and would most likely have won in 1971 had he not crashed (see The Agony of Ocaña, page 136). He retired in 1977, but was dogged by bad luck including a failed business venture, two car crashes, and developing hepatitis after a botched blood transfusion. When his wife left him it was the final straw for Ocaña, who shot himself at his home in the French town of Mont-de-Marsan.

1995: DEATH OF A BIKE RIDER

In 1995 Miguel Indurain stormed to his record-equalling fifth Tour de France victory. But even this magnificent achievement was over-shadowed by the tragic death of Italian rider Fabio Casartelli on the perilous slopes of the Portet-d'Aspet in the Pyrenees. Casartelli was the 25-year-old winner of the gold medal at the Barcelona Olympics in 1992 and in this, only his second Tour, he was hoping to build on an already burgeoning reputation as a top-class rider. It's not clear precisely what happened: all that is known is that several riders lost control on one of the hairpin bends and Casartelli smashed head-first into one of the unforgiving granite blocks protecting the edge of the road. He was not wearing a helmet, and his injuries were severe. TV images showed him curled into a foetal position on the tarmac with rivulets of blood pouring down the road. He was airlifted to hospital in Tarbes, unconscious, but his heart stopped three times on the way, and shortly after his arrival Casartelli was pronounced dead.

The profound shock of his death affected the peloton, and in particular his friend and team-mate Lance Armstrong. Two days later Armstrong won the stage into Limoges, pointing his fingers to the heavens in tribute to his fallen comrade as he crossed the line. In broader terms, the manner of Casartelli's death would lead to the mandatory wearing of helmets in the Tour.

TOUR TRIVIA

Luc Leblanc, who came fifth overall in the 1995 Tour, has one leg that's 3 inches shorter than the other as a result of a childhood accident.

1995: FIVE FOR BIG MIG

The death of Fabio Casartelli cast a shadow across the Tour de France in 1995, but it didn't stop Miguel Indurain from conducting business as usual on the way to winning his fifth Tour. Once again the Spaniard's dominance of the first time trial gave him an unassailable lead midway through the race, which he was able to defend in the mountains and increase in the final time trial. His victory meant he was the first man to win the Tour on five consecutive occasions – a magnificent achievement, but an ominous one. Quite simply Indurain was unbeatable, and there seemed no end to the number of Tours he could win. Of more concern to the organisers was the fact the race had become yawn-makingly predictable. Indurain's modus operandi was to win effectively and unspectacularly, reserving his efforts for the time trials and happy to allow others to win stages as long as it did not affect his overall lead. It was hardly conducive to riveting TV – but other than let down his tyres, what could they do?

They need not have worried: the Tour had broken unbeatable riders before and, as Indurain would soon discover, it would break him as well.

TOUR STALWARTS (MOST NUMBER OF TOURS)

16: Joop Zoetemelk (HOL)
15: Lucien Van Impe (BEL), Guy Nulens (BEL)
14: Viatcheslav Ekimov (RUS), Raymond Poulidor (FRA), Sean Kelly (IRL), André Darrigade (FRA)

'If [Indurain] had been a ploughman, he'd have taken care to plough the perfect furrow. And he'd have adapted perfectly to such a life because it would have been healthy, and he would have been just as happy at the end of the long working day.'

L'Équipe pays homage to Big Mig

TOUR TRIVIA

In 2000 Chris Boardman attempted to break Eddy Merckx's distance of 30.64 miles (49.31 km) for the hour record, using the same type of stainless steel bike that the Belgian had used 28 years earlier. He did it — by just 10 metres.

☆ TOUR STARS WHO DIED IN 1995

Marcel Bidot, aged 93: As a rider Bidot contested six Tours between 1926 and 1932, finishing fifth in 1930. But it was as French team manager in the 1950s and 1960s that Bidot was better known. In that time he oversaw such stars as Bobet, Anquetil, Pingeon, Darrigade, Rivière and Poulidor. He was famed for writing his team selections on the back of Gitanes cigarette packets, so much so that the French tobacco producers paid him 100,000 francs for all the publicity they reckoned he'd brought them.

1996: THE LEADEN HAND OF FATE

There comes a time in every great champion's career when the tipping point is reached and an irreversible decline sets in. Usually it is a gentle decline into retirement over a season or two. But sometimes it happens in the blink of an eye. It happened to Merckx on the Pra-Loup in 1975 (see I Eat Cannibal, page 143), and in 1991 Miguel Indurain watched as Greg Lemond abruptly cracked on the slopes of the Col du Tourmalet (see The King Is Dead, Long Live The King, page 184). In 1996 it happened to the great Spaniard himself on the road to Les Arcs, high in the Alps, on stage seven of that year's Tour. Following the leaders, and showing no sign of distress as he approached the final couple of kilometres, Indurain's stony face suddenly twisted into a grimace of pain. It seemed impossible, but yes! Big Mig was actually *struggling* to keep up! He eventually finished a whopping four minutes behind the stage winner, Luc Leblanc, but even then few believed that it was nothing other than a bad day at the office for the five-times winner. The next day Indurain finished fifth in the time trial, and even his most fervent fans knew the game was up. He would finish the race with the stragglers, and his eventual eleventh place in the general classification was his lowest position in a Tour de France since 1989. Indurain was canny enough to ensure it would also be his last.

Vive le Tour!

1996: ARMSTRONG ABANDONS

The previous year Lance Armstrong had provided the memorable image
of the Tour with his homage to his dead team-mate Fabio Casartelli at
the end of the Limoges stage. In 1996 it was a very different story as he
abandoned in the rain, drained of energy and unable to continue. Two
months later, a medical examination would reveal that his body was
riddled with cancer and doctors would give the young American only a
50–50 chance of survival.

1996: THE RIIS STUFF

Bjarne who? That was the reaction of much of the cycling world to Bjarne
Riis's surprise Tour de France win in 1996. While everyone else was waiting
for Miguel Indurain to sweep to his record-breaking sixth victory, the Dane
nipped in and clinched first place while the big man faltered on the slopes
and in the time trials. Riis was an unlikely Tour champion in many ways. Tall
and balding, at the age of 32 his career highlights consisted of a couple of
Tour stage wins and victory in the Tour of Denmark. But the previous year
he had finished third and briefly worn the *maillot jaune*, so it could be
argued that in the absence of Indurain he could be included among the
challengers. Riis took his chance with both hands. His victory was carved
out in the Alps, on a normally tortuous mountain stage to Sestriere that was
shortened to just 28 miles (46 km) due to snow on the cols of the Iseran
and the Galibier. Riis won the stage, and the yellow jersey, by 28 seconds
from Indurain. Later in the Pyrenees, Riis emphasised the fact that this was
his year by winning another stage – the first yellow jersey to win a massed-
start stage since Laurent Fignon seven years earlier.

☆ TOUR STARS WHO DIED IN 1996

Roger Lapébie, aged 85: Lapébie won the Tour in 1937, but his victory was clouded in controversy after he was found to have taken a tow from team cars in the mountains (see When Push Comes to Shove, page 59).

Hubert Opperman, aged 91: 'Oppy', as he was known, was an Australian who rode the Tour in 1928 and 1931 after a campaign by the *Melbourne Herald* to get antipodean riders included in the race. He finished a creditable eighteenth and twelfth, respectively. In later life, Oppy became Australian minister of transport, and later High Commissioner to Malta. He remained a passionate cyclist, however, and only quit riding his bike on doctors' advice at the age of 90. A year later he died of a heart attack while riding his static exercise bike.

TOUR TRIVIA

Coverage of the Tour is provided by French TV. Each year they have over 300 people working on the live broadcast, including four helicopters, two aircraft, three motorcycles, four race cars, and 20 roadside cameras. Its pictures are beamed to 160 countries and over 100 million viewers – making the Tour the third largest sporting event after the Olympics and the World Cup.

1997: BRILLIANT BOARDMAN

Three years after winning the Prologue on his first attempt, Britain's Chris Boardman did it again, this time taking the yellow jersey on the 4.5 mile (7.3 km) sprint in Rouen by two seconds. It was a welcome return for Boardman, who in 1995 had fallen during a rainswept stage and been run over by his own support car, suffering a broken ankle. As we shall see, it was not the last time the unlucky Scouser would be dogged by disaster.

THE CRAZY WORLD OF MARIO CIPOLLINI

Cycling has never been short of extroverts, but there has never been anyone to compare with Mario Cipollini. Known variously as 'Cipo', 'Super Mario' and latterly 'The Lion King', the Italian sprint specialist delighted the crowds as much as he annoyed the Tour organisers. His policy was straightforward: compete in the early sprints, win as many high-profile stages as possible, then jump off the bike as soon as the race approached the mountains. Between 1992 and 1999 Cipo rode seven Tours and never completed one of them. Instead, he used his brief appearances to Infuriated, Tour director Jean-Marie Leblanc prevented Cipo from competing in 2001 and 2002 by banning his team from the event. It made little difference to Cipo, who continued to amaze and outrage up until his retirement in 2005.

Some of his career highlights, on and off the bike, include:

Dressing up as an ancient Roman during a rest day in the 1999 Tour to celebrate his record successive stage win.

Wearing a selection of garish sprinting skin-suits, including: muscle suit, zebra pattern, and techno design inspired by the movie *Tron*.

Wearing different coloured shorts every day of the 1997 Tour, and being subsequently fined every day.

Wearing a green jersey with the word 'Peace' across the chest during the 1998 Prologue in Ireland.

Filling his wardrobe with hundreds of suits, ties and shoes – most of which he admitted he'd never worn.

Claiming to have stopped midway through a stage to 'perform a sex act' on a podium girl.

Claiming that, 'If I wasn't a professional cyclist, I'd be a porn star', and, 'I want to die in an orgy.'

Using his mobile phone to call a friend midway through a stage.

Appearing next to a stripper called Cleopatra at the start of the 1999 Tour.

Riding a stage of the Tour with a photo of Pamela Anderson on his handlebars.

Getting arrested for training on the *autostrada* near his home in Lucca. He told police it was the only way he could safely get to his top speed.

Journalist Matt Rendell summed it up when he described Cipollini thus: 'Over 25 years, Mario has taken a physique blessed with innate physical gifts and moulded it into a ruthless sprinting machine. Part of this relentlessly single-minded project has been to refuse even to begin the mountain stages of major tours in order to protect his muscle shape. Any improvement in climbing would jeopardise his pure speed. That means near invincibility in his ideal race profile – the long, flat sprint finish where victory depends on positional sense, a high-speed lead-out, and blinding maximum speed – but vulnerability where matters are complicated by no more than a few curves, a slight gradient, and a cross-wind. And as a stage racer, Super Mario doesn't even register on the screen.'

1997: JAN THE MAN

In 1996, Jan Ullrich dedicated himself to the service of Telekom team-mate Bjarne Riis. The following year the young East German-born rider made it very clear that even though Riis was the reigning champion, a new gun was in town. In the Pyrenees, red-haired Ullrich destroyed the field on a punishing climb up to Arcalis in Andorra, and a couple of days later, wearing yellow, he won the 34 mile (55 km) time trial in St Etienne in convincing style to reinforce his lead. He would arrive in Paris more than nine minutes ahead of Richard Virenque, his nearest rival, with former champion Riis trailing in seventh, 26 minutes behind. At 23 years of age, Ullrich had become the first German to win the Tour de France, and the manner of his victory suggested it would be the first of many. Across in Texas, however, another rider had different ideas.

1997: PANTANI TAMES THE ALPE

In 1994 infrared sensors were installed at either end of the 21-hairpin climb to the summit of Alpe d'Huez in order to record the fastest ascents. That year the tiny Italian climber Marco Pantani completed the 9 miles (14.5 km) in just 37 minutes 15 seconds. Quite how good this time is can be gauged by the fact that the only person to beat it is Pantani himself, in 1997 when he recorded 36 minutes 55 seconds, and in 1995 when he set the record for the fastest ascent with an astonishing 36 minutes 50 seconds. What makes Pantani's achievement even greater is that in 1999 the official climb was actually shortened to 8.6 miles (14 km). Lance Armstrong's time of 37 minutes 36 seconds in the 2004 time trial remains the nearest anyone has come to Pantani's time.

'I've spent my whole career knowing I'll never win the Tour, so I rely on my media value. If I do something, it gets in the papers. Sometimes, 100 km of riding alone in the Tour de France has more significance than a win in another race.'

Jacky Durand – the French rider breakaway king who never finished higher than 65th in the ten Tours he competed in between 1992 and 2002 – explains his philosophy for Tour immortality

Vive le Tour!

TOUR LEADERS WHO ABANDONED

Francis Pélissier, illness, 1927

Victor Fontan, broken bike, 1929

Sylvère Maes, abuse from French spectators, 1937

Fiorenzo Magni, abuse from French spectators, 1950

Wim van Est, crashed into a ravine, 1951

Bernard van de Kerckhove, illness, 1965

Luis Ocaña, crashed and hit by other riders, 1971

Michel Pollentier, failed dope test, 1978

Bernard Hinault, knee injury, 1980

Pascal Simon, broken collarbone (although he did continue for six days afterwards), 1983

Rolf Sorensen, broken collarbone, 1991

Stephane Heulot, knee injury, 1996

Chris Boardman, crashed into a wall, 1998

HITCHING A RIDE

The unforgettable images of the Tour are provided by a team of motorcycle cameramen who follow the action wherever it leads them. While the driver weaves through the peloton, the cameraman must perch on the back, usually facing the wrong way, in order to get the close-up shots of suffering that are beamed around the world.

☆ TOUR STARS WHO DIED IN 1997

Fritz Schaer, aged 71: Swiss-born Schaer was the first winner of the green 'points' jersey in 1957.

EPO

First it was strong liquor and cocaine, then amphetamines, then steroids. By the late 1980s the drug of choice among the professional peloton was EPO – erythropoietin, to give it its full name. In layman's terms, EPO is a hormone which increases red blood cells and thereby enables the blood to carry more oxygen to the muscles. It was originally developed as a treatment for patients undergoing blood transfusions, but it wasn't long before the benefits to long-distance athletes were picked up by unscrupulous coaches and doctors. Cyclists, and in particular those involved in gruelling, three-week stage races, discovered that EPO offsets the natural decrease in red blood cells, allowing them to perform at a higher level and for longer. Its undetected use would certainly explain a number of spectacular displays of endurance. In 1997 the Italian star Claudio Chiappucci was caught using blood-doping products, leading to suggestions that his legendary solo break to Sestriere in 1992 may have had more to do with what was in his bloodstream than in his legs.

In the end, the existence of EPO came to the attention of the cycling authorities not through the unusually brilliant performances of riders, but rather due to their mysterious deaths. A sinister side-effect of the drug is that it can produce so many red blood cells that the blood effectively turns to porridge, clogging the arteries and leading to heart attacks. This commonly happens at night when the body is at rest – which has led to the unedifying sight of doped riders setting their alarms to go off every couple of hours so they can leap out of bed and get their circulation going again.

However, it was not until 1998 that the full extent of EPO use in the professional peloton was revealed, as the drug users and the anti-doping authorities headed for an inevitable showdown that would threaten the very existence of the Tour de France.

'You feel as though your kidneys are two balloons of water flopping around the base of your back. Your joints ache and you have trouble seeing.'

Erwan Mentheour, former Tour rider, describes the effects of EPO

YOUNGEST TOUR WINNERS

19 years: Henri Cornet (FRA) in 1904
21 years, 10 months: Romain Maes (BEL) in 1935
22 years, 6 months: François Faber (LUX) in 1909
22 years, 9 months: Octave Lapize (FRA) in 1910
22 years, 10 months: Felice Gimondi (ITA) in 1965
22 years, 11 months: Laurent Fignon (FRA) in 1983

1998: PANTANI WINS THE TOUR OF SHAME

The 1998 Tour was won, against the odds, by Marco Pantani. The flyweight Italian climber, who had recovered from a horrific collision with a car in 1995 in which one of his legs was broken in three places, inflicted a devastating defeat on reigning champion Jan Ullrich in the climb to Les Deux Alpes, and rode into Paris with a lead of three minutes. With his bandana and earring, Pantani styled himself as *Il Pirata* – the Pirate – and there is no doubt that his image, along with his superlative climbing ability, breathed new life into a Tour that had become dominated by muscular time-triallists. But then the 1998 Tour was completed by just 96 riders. One team had been disqualified, another was under investigation, and the race had been disrupted by two rider strikes to the extent that at one stage it was doubtful it would ever reach Paris. Pantani won, and won deservedly. But it was his misfortune that he would be known as the winner of the Tour of Shame, the one wrecked by what would become known as the Festina Affair.

FEEDING FRENZY:

A Tour rider can expend over 8,000 calories a day - which is why their daily food intake has to be vast.

1998: THE FESTINA AFFAIR

Drugs and drug-takers had been the unspoken evil of the Tour ever since the war – although in the case of great champions like Fausto Coppi and Jacques Anquetil, it was an accepted part of being a top-class cyclist. As time passed, however, attitudes changed; and when the likes of Merckx and Hinault proved that greatness could be achieved without a syringe, opinion hardened against the dopers. Cycling became the most rigorously tested sport in the world, and offenders were punished accordingly. Yet the suspicion remained that within this murky world, the professional peloton and the teams that controlled it were still giving the authorities the runaround.

The events of July 1998 shattered any illusion that cycling had cleaned up its act. If anything, the so-called Festina Affair showed to the world just how rotten the sport had become. It certainly revealed that the extent and sophistication of the techniques used to drug riders were far in excess of anything the anti-doping authorities had ever imagined.

The timetable of events unfolded as follows:

July 8: Willy Voet, masseur for the French Festina team of four-times King of the Mountains Richard Virenque and World Champion Laurent Brochard, is arrested on the French-Belgian border. In his car are 400 vials of various drugs, including anabolic steroids and EPO.

July 11: The Tour de France Prologue in Dublin is won by Britain's Chris Boardman. Festina riders and management are present. They dismiss the allegations against Voet, claiming he was acting alone.

July 13: Stage two, Eniscorthy–Cork. Under questioning, Voet claims he was acting under the instructions of Festina team manager Bruno Roussel and doctor Eric Rijckaert.

July 15: Stage four, Plouay–Cholet. Roussel and Rijckaert are arrested.

July 16: Stage five, Cholet–Chateauroux. The Union Cycliste International (UCI) suspends Roussel's management licence.

July 17: Stage six, La Châtre–Brive. Roussel admits to allowing drugs to be administered to his riders under 'controlled medical supervision'. Five Festina riders confess to taking drugs. Festina are kicked out of the Tour. In a televised statement, Tour director Jean-Marie Leblanc said that Roussel's admission 'appeared terrible to us…because it was more or less a confession…that doping has been endemic in the Festina team and that the team organised it. For the sake of the Tour de France, for cycling, we hope that we can put an end to the atmosphere of suspicion that has reigned over this event since the start in Dublin.'

July 24: Stage twelve, Tarascon-sur-Ariège–Cap d'Agde. The peloton goes on strike, sitting in the road at the stage start in protest at the persecution of the Festina team.

July 28: Stage sixteen, Vizille–Albertville. The doctor and team director of the TVM team are hauled in for questioning.

July 29: Stage seventeen, Albertville–Aix-les-Bains. Riders go on strike again in support of the TVM team.

In all, almost 30 people were arrested and questioned over the Festina

Affair. The inquiry dragged on for several months. Richard Virenque, who had always denied doping, finally admitted it and was banned for nine months. Those who had come clean immediately were suspended for six. The sport of cycling and its showpiece event had been dragged through the mud, but now it had been purged and claimed that it was clean. Few observers were convinced. As it approached the new century and its own one 100th anniversary, what cycling and the Tour de France in particular needed was someone who it could hold up as a shining example of what the sport stood for. It needed a new Bartali, a new Merckx. In short, it was holding out for a hero…

TOUR WINNERS 1986–1998

1986: Greg Lemond (USA), [KoM: Bernard Hinault (FRA); Points: Eric Vanderaerden (BEL)]

1987: Stephen Roche (IRE), [KoM: Luis Herrera (COL); Points: Jean-Paul van Poppel (NED)]

1988: Pedro Delgado (SPA), [KoM: Steven Rooks (NED); Points: Eddy Plankaert (BEL)]

1989: Greg Lemond (USA), [KoM: Gert-Jan Theunisse (NED); Points: Sean Kelly (IRE)]

1990: Greg Lemond (USA), [KoM: Thierry Claveyrolat (FRA); Points: Olaf Ludwig (GER)]

1991: Miguel Indurain (SPA), [KoM: Claudio Chiappucci (ITA); Points:

Vive le Tour!

Djamolidine Abdoujaparov (USSR)]

1992: Miguel Indurain (SPA), [KoM: Claudio Chiappucci (ITA); Points: Laurent Jalabert (FRA)]

1993: Miguel Indurain (SPA), [KoM: Tony Rominger (SWI); Points: Djamolidine Abdoujaparov (USSR)]

1994: Miguel Indurain (SPA), [KoM: Richard Virenque (FRA); Points: Djamolidine Abdoujaparov (USSR)]

1995: Miguel Indurain (SPA), [KoM: Richard Virenque (FRA); Points: Laurent Jalabert (FRA)]

1996: Bjarne Riis (DEN), [KoM: Richard Virenque (FRA); Points: Erik Zabel (GER)]

1997: Jan Ullrich (GER), [KoM: Richard Virenque (FRA); Points: Erik Zabel (GER)]

1998: Marco Pantani (ITA), [KoM: Christophe Rinero (FRA), Points: Erik Zabel (GER)]

ARMSTRONG: THE RISE OF THE MACHINE 1999–2006

'All the teams in Europe that had offered me contracts before my cancer turned me down after I had recovered. They said I was damaged goods.'

Lance Armstrong, cancer survivor and seven-times winner of the Tour de France

ANATOMY OF A LEGEND: LANCE ARMSTRONG

Born in Plano, Texas, on 18 September 1971, Armstrong came from a broken home and was brought up by his mother. He claims bike riding was the only thing that prevented him from going off the rails into a life of crime and drugs.

He originally started out as a triathlete, competing in adult competitions from the age of just fourteen and becoming national junior champion.

At the age of seventeen Armstrong was invited to train with the US Junior National Cycling Team. His mother gave her blessing for him to drop out of high school in order to train.

In 1991 Armstrong won the US amateur championship. A year later he finished fourteenth in the Barcelona Olympics road race and turned professional.

Vive le Tour!

The future seven-times Tour winner had an inauspicious start to his professional career, finishing last in the San Sebastian Classic. Despite being ordered to abandon the race by his team, Armstrong insisted on finishing, crossing the line as the organisers were packing away the winners' podium. He later claimed that if he'd abandoned, he would have retired from the sport.

Things soon started to look up for Armstrong: the following year he stunned the cycling world by winning the World Championship in Oslo. Invited afterwards to meet the King of Norway, he initially refused because his mother had not been invited. The King quickly changed his mind.

As a member of the Motorola team, Armstrong won stages of the Tour de France in 1993 and 1995.

In 1996 he was forced to abandon the Tour due to ill-health. Three months later, on 2 October, he checked into a hospital in Austin, Texas, complaining of a painful groin. Doctors diagnosed testicular cancer that had already spread to his stomach and lungs and was now threatening his brain. They gave him little more than a 40 per cent chance of survival – although they later admitted that the real figure was nearer 3 per cent.

His treatment involved surgery to remove both testicles and lesions on his brain. Warned that chemotherapy would ultimately impair his lung function and effectively end his career as a top cyclist, Armstrong opted for more aggressive treatment that would affect his lungs less.

To everyone's amazement, Armstrong not only survived the cancer but was well enough to resume training the following year. To his disgust, however, he had been dropped by the Cofidis team that had signed him prior to his cancer diagnosis. The newly formed US Postal Service team stepped in to sign him.

Soon after his recovery, Armstrong set up the Lance Armstrong Foundation, aimed at supporting cancer victims and raising awareness of the disease. A symbol of the Foundation was the yellow Livestrong wristband, sold (at £1 each in the UK) to raise money for cancer research. By the end of 2006 more than 65 million of these wristbands had been sold around the world. Armstrong himself became a member of George W. Bush's President's Cancer Panel in 2002.

In 1998 Armstrong married girlfriend Kristin. Together they had three children: Luke, and twins Isabelle and Grace, through IVF treatment. In 2003 the couple filed for divorce, and that same year Armstrong began dating singer Sheryl Crow. Matchmakers were disappointed, however, when in 2006 Armstrong and Crow announced they were to split.

Armstrong's celebrity has made him one of the most recognised sportsmen on the planet. His book *It's Not About the Bike* was voted William Hill Sports Book of the Year in 2000.

Despite strenuous efforts to prove that Armstrong took performance enhancing drugs during his career, the American only once tested positive for a doping product. In 1999, the year of his comeback, his urine was found to contain corticosteroids, although the amount was not in the positive test range. He later produced a medical certificate proving that the substance was contained in a cream he was using to counter saddle sores.

Armstrong for President? Since his retirement, Armstrong has hinted that he might be interested in a career in politics, and it is rumoured that he will one day stand for Governor of Texas.

TOUR TRIVIA

In 1999 the Italian rider Beppe Guerini was racing to victory on the Alpe d'Huez when a spectator with a camera stepped out in front of him. The two collided and Guerini hit the deck. The spectator, known only as Eric, helped him back onto his bike and Guerini continued on his way to win the stage. Later that evening, Eric went to Guerini's hotel to apologise.

Vive le Tour!

MOST PODIUM FINISHES

8: Raymond Poulidor (FRA), came second three times, third five times
7: Joop Zoetemelk (HOL), won once, came second six times; Lance
Armstrong (USA), won seven times; Jan Ullrich (GER), won once,
came second five times, third once
6: Bernard Hinault (FRA), won 5 times, came second once; Eddy
Merckx (BEL), won five times, came second once

TOUR TRIVIA
The modern Tour consists of 21 teams, each containing nine riders.
Fifteen of the teams are selected automatically through their UCI
ranking; the remaining six are wild-card selections chosen by members
of the Tour organising committee.

1999: THE DRUGS DON'T WORK

Marco Pantani was the man who emerged unscathed from the
wreckage of the 1998 *Tour de Dopage* – the little Italian climber crowned
champion after a stunning performance in the high mountains, seen by
many as a beacon of hope in the morass of drug cheats. Yet on the
morning of 5 June 1999, with the implications of the Festina scandal
still rumbling, it was announced by the organisers of the Giro d'Italia
that Pantani – just one day away from winning the event for a second
successive year – had tested positive for EPO. Despite his vehement and
tearful protests, Pantani was booted out of the Giro and consequently
banned from that year's Tour de France. With former champion Jan
Ullrich out of the race with a knee injury, it seemed the 1999 Tour had

been shorn of favourites and was anybody's race. One man who was not thought to be in contention was Lance Armstrong, who just three years earlier had been on his deathbed. But the Texan, now almost unrecognisable from the stocky, headstrong rider who had bulldozed to two stage wins in 1993 and 1995, had other ideas. The Armstrong era was about to begin.

BROKEN COLLARBONE

The most common injury among cyclists is a broken collarbone, usually sustained following a high-speed crash. Such an injury usually means an enforced rest of up to one month. In 2003, however, America's Tyler Hamilton broke his collarbone in a crash on the first stage of the Tour – but insisted on strapping it up and finishing the race, gritting his teeth through the pain to win stage sixteen.

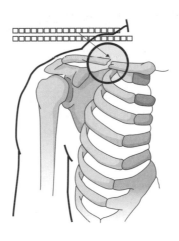

1999: BASSONS SPEAKS OUT

Christophe Bassons of France was an honest, hard-working pro whose one and only Tour was in 1999. The reason for this is that university-educated Bassons dared to speak out about the drugs problem he still believed infected the sport of cycling a year after the Festina scandal. Pointing out that there was nothing natural about average speeds in excess of 31 mph (50 kph) on flat stages, Bassons made it clear that in his opinion many riders were still using performance-enhancing drugs. Breaking the unspoken code made him hugely unpopular in the peloton, and at one stage Lance Armstrong sought him out on the road and told Bassons what he thought of him. A couple of days later, after more threats, he packed his bag and told his team boss that he was quitting the race. The following year Bassons published a book about his experience, entitled *Positif*. He never raced again.

Bassons' story echoes that of Irish rider Paul Kimmage, who in 1990 wrote a book called *Rough Ride* which detailed the extent of doping in the peloton. Although the book became a best-seller, Kimmage was ostracised by his peers including his old friend and countryman Stephen Roche. Kimmage, now a journalist, maintains that the drug problem has been swept under the carpet, and prior to the 2006 Tour voiced his suspicions once again about some of the top riders. A few days later Jan Ullrich, Ivan Basso and several leading contenders were kicked out of the Tour on the eve of the Prologue, and eventual winner Floyd Landis tested positive for testosterone after the race.

NUMBER OF STAGE WINS

34: Eddy Merckx
28: Bernard Hinault
25: André Leducq
22: André Darrigade, Lance Armstrong
20: Nicolas Frantz
19: François Faber
17: Jean Alavoine
16: Charles Pélissier, Jacques Anquetil, René Le Grèves
13: Louis Trousselier
12: Miguel Indurain, Jean Aerts, Mario Cipollini, Gino Bartali, Erik Zabel
11: Louison Bobet, Raffaele Di Paco
10: Charly Gaul, Jan Raas, Maurice Archambaud, Henri Pélissier, Walter Godefroot, Joop Zoetemelk, Gerrie Knetemann

1999: CIPO DOES IT AGAIN

Amid all the gloom of drug cheats and expelled riders, one man could be relied upon to raise the spirits. Sure enough, the larger-than-life Italian sprinter Mario Cipollini blasted to four consecutive stage wins in his own inimitable style. Whether he was dressing up as a Roman to celebrate Caesar's birthday with a stripper dressed as Cleopatra, calling up a mate on his mobile phone while speeding along in the peloton, or being fined for his array of colourful and illegal skin suits (see The Crazy World of Mario Cipollini, page 203), Cipo's dominance of the sprints could not be denied. On the 118 mile (191 km) stage from Laval to Blois, he and his lead-out team set a record average speed of 31.29 mph (50.355 kph).

Vive le Tour!

999: ROAD TO HELL

For much of the day, the causeway of the Passage de Gois, which connects the French mainland to the island of Noirmoutier in western France, is underwater. When it is not, the narrow pathway is a treacherous strip of slippery cobbles – just as it was the day the peloton passed over it during an early stage of the 1999 Tour. Sure enough, the Passage was the scene of a mass pile-up of riders and bikes in which many of the favourites – including the eventual second-placed Alex Zulle of Switzerland – lost upwards of six minutes from the leading group as they disentangled themselves. Among that leading group was Lance Armstrong, and it's arguable that this crash was pivotal in securing his first Tour win.

999: TIME-TRIAL SUPREMO

Armstrong had already set out his stall by winning the Tour Prologue in Le Puy-du-Fou. Although he would consolidate his lead at the Metz time trial a week later, the following day he destroyed renowned climbers like Alex Zulle, Fernando Escartín of Spain, and four times King of the Mountains Richard Virenque on the gruelling Alpine climb up to Sestriere. Here, once again, was an all-rounder in the mould of Anquetil – a man who was unbeatable on the flat and unstoppable in the mountains.

IT'S ALL ABOUT CADENCE

Cadence is the term given to the number of pedal revolutions a cyclist completes in a minute. On a mountain climb, the usual cadence is 70–90 revolutions per minute (rpm). Following his cancer treatment, Lance Armstrong's coaches decided that he was too weak to push big gears, so they modified his technique so that he would push a smaller gear at a far higher cadence. Thus it was that the American was able to climb mountains at over 120 rpm, enabling him to dart away from his churning rivals at will.

1999: C'EST SUSPICIOUS, NON?

After his prolonged cancer treatment there was perhaps understandably a great deal of suspicion that Lance Armstrong's victory in the 1999 Tour had been achieved with the help of performance-enhancing drugs. Armstrong vehemently denied the charge, and every anti-doping test proved negative. It was to be a routine that would continue throughout his career. The American pointed out that his body mass had changed substantially during his chemotherapy, as had his training methods subsequently. He was now a lean and honed cycling machine as opposed to the stocky former triathlete pre-1996. It is also worth noting that his 1999 victory made Armstrong only the second American after Greg Lemond to win the Tour – and Lemond had come back from his own deathbed to win a decade earlier.

Shortest:
Samuel Dumoulin (FRA)
born August 1980
1.58 m (5ft 2in)

Tallest:
Johan Van Summeren (BEL)
born Feb 1981
1.98 m (6ft 5.5in)

TALL AND SHORT

Cyclists come in all shapes and sizes. This was illustrated during the 2005 Tour, which featured two of the tallest and shortest riders ever to appear in the peloton.

TOUR TRIVIA

The *Étape du Tour* is an annual event in which amateur cyclists ride a stage of the Tour de France a couple of days before the professionals. From humble beginnings, the *Étape* now attracts over 8,000 club riders from all over the world, eager to test themselves on such legendary climbs as the Alpe d'Huez. While most take a leisurely ten to twelve hours to complete the route, the *Étape* is also regarded as a good opportunity for ambitious amateurs to show themselves. The winner of the first *Étape* in 1997 was Frenchman Christophe Rinero, who went on to win the King of the Mountains in the Tour of 1998.

TOUR TRIVIA

Was French suspicion of Lance Armstrong motivated by their own disappointment? The 1999 Tour was the first for 70 years in which a Frenchman failed to win a stage of his own blue riband event.

☆ TOUR STARS WHO DIED IN 1999

Thierry Claveyrolat, aged 40: The Frenchman competed in nine Tours between 1985 and 1993, but although he won King of the Mountains in 1990 he never finished higher than 21st. Having retired to run a bar in Grenoble, Claveyrolat was involved in a car crash in which a family of four was critically injured. He sank into deep depression, and in September 1999 shot himself at his home.

TOUR TRIVIA

The Colombian climber Luis Herrera retired a rich man in 1992, and became even wealthier through his cattle business back home. In 2000 he was kidnapped by the Revolutionary Army Force of Colombia and was forced to pay an unspecified amount to secure his freedom 20 hours later.

2000: GRAND PLANS, GREAT RESULT FOR MILLAR

Many grand ideas were suggested to celebrate the first Tour de France of the new millennium. Top of the list was to transport the teams and accompanying caravan across the Atlantic for a spectacular *Grand Départ* in New York. Once the cost of such an enterprise was worked out, however, the plan was quickly shelved. Instead, the Tour began in Paris, at the horrendous modern eyesore of the Futuroscope theme park near Poitiers. If this vision of the future was supposed to inspire the French riders to a long-overdue success, it failed dismally. The 10 mile (16.5 km) Prologue was won by the young Scots rider David Millar, who pipped returning champion Lance Armstrong by two seconds and held the yellow jersey for three days.

NICKED – IN 50 YEARS TIME

In the run-up to the 2000 Tour de France, the event organisers made the curious announcement that this year all anti-doping urine samples would be frozen. Then, when a reliable method of detecting EPO had been invented, the samples would be thawed and tested. This gave rise to the odd prospect of long-retired riders being hauled over the coals for doping offences they had committed decades ago.

TOUR TRIVIA

For winning the Tour, a rider can expect a prize of around €400,000 (£250,000). Traditionally, he then distributes this money among his team-mates.

2000: WINNERS UNITED . . . IN DEFEAT

If Armstrong's win in 1999 can be attributed to the fact that both the previous two winners of the Tour – Jan Ullrich and Marco Pantani were missing, then there was no excuse in 2000 as both men returned fully fit and raring to go. In the event, their challenge was disappointingly fleeting, a pattern that in Ullrich's case would become standard practice for the next six years. A Pantani attack on the road to Hautacam was swallowed up by the American almost before it began, while Ullrich could only benefit by two minutes when Armstrong appeared to crack in the Alps. In the final time trial in Germany, which Ullrich was expected to win, Armstrong set a new Tour record of 33.25 mph (53.986 kph). The American sailed into Paris with a comfortable six minute lead over Ullrich, his second Tour victory assured.

2000: THE PISSPOT REBELLION

It is a little-known rule outside of the peloton that when the man in the yellow jersey decides he needs to answer the call of nature, the rest of the pack do not launch attacks. In 2000, the field were just 6 miles (10 km) from the stage start at Vitré when race leader Laurent Jalabert was caught short. As he paused by the roadside, up ahead big Magnus Backstedt, the British-adopted Swede, decided to set off on a break. Whether he knew about Jalabert or not – and he later claimed he didn't – is irrelevant. Backstedt's break was joined by several others and by the time Jalabert was back on his bike, the group were far away down the road. Despite a chase by Jalabert's ONCE team, it quickly became clear that the Backstedt group would not be caught. As a result, Jalabert lost more than seven minutes on the stage, and with it the yellow jersey. He and Backstedt are still not speaking.

TOUR TRIVIA

In 2000, 60 per cent of bike frames were made from aluminium, 25 per cent from carbon, and 15 per cent from a mixture of the two. It was the first time that stainless steel had not been used by Tour riders.

2000: HATS OFF TO DUMBO

Marco Pantani may not have challenged Lance Armstrong for the yellow jersey in 2000, but the Italian was involved in one of the few noteworthy incidents in an otherwise dull race. Stage twelve was a long battle through Provence that ended at the summit of Mont Ventoux. With just a few kilometres to go, only Armstrong and Pantani were left to duel for victory on the pitiless barren slopes where Tom Simpson had died 33 years earlier. As the two men reached the summit, Armstrong appeared to slow down, allowing Pantani the victory. Already safe in yellow, this is indeed what Armstrong claimed after the stage. Pantani was incensed by this, claiming that if this was true then it betrayed a lack of respect by the American. In response, Armstrong called Pantani *Elefantino* – Italian for 'Dumbo' – a direct reference to the Italian's prominent ears. Although Armstrong later apologised, Pantani was never the forgiving type and the two men entered into a feud that would last until the Italian's untimely death four years later.

'It's a shame he [Armstrong] has no concept of the tremendous history there is to cycling, because he came to it from triathlon and I'm sure that influences the way he sees the sport.'

George Mount, 1970s American cyclist

2000: FIST-FIGHT FURORE

Having slogged round France for three long weeks, in 2000 the Dutch rider Jeroen Blijlevens was disqualified within seconds of the finish in Paris after thumping the American Bobby Julich. The two had been niggling at each other throughout the Tour and as they crossed the finish line, Blijlevens lost his cool and started pushing and verbally abusing Julich. Julich responded by throwing his helmet at the Dutchman, and a fight broke out in which Julich ended up with a cut lip. Blijlevens was found to be to blame, disqualified from the Tour and banned for a month.

MOST DAYS IN YELLOW

96: Eddy Merckx
83: Lance Armstrong
78: Bernard Hinault
60: Miguel Indurain
51: Jacques Anquetil
39: Antonin Magne
37: Nicolas Frantz

35: André Leducq
34: Louison Bobet
33: Ottavio Bottecchia
26: Romain Maes, Sylvère Maes, René Vietto
22: Laurent Fignon, Joop Zoetemelk, Greg Lemond
20: Gino Bartali

2001: ARMSTRONG'S BLUFF

In 2001 Lance Armstrong seemed very content to sit back and allow the also-rans to scrap for recognition on the flat stages before the mountains. Yet as soon as the peloton reached the 6,123 ft (1,924 m) Col du Glandon in the Alps, it seemed that the superman was human after all. To the amazement of everyone – not least his big rival Jan Ullrich – Armstrong's face was twisted in pain and he was clearly struggling. Sniffing their opportunity to kick a man while he was down, Ullrich and his Telekom team went hell-for-leather for the Alpe d'Huez. Somehow Armstrong clung on to the foot of the 21 hairpins. Then, astonishingly, the American began to edge past Ullrich. Then came a moment which would go down in Tour legend, as Armstrong turned in his saddle and stared long and hard into the German's eyes before setting off up the road at a blistering pace. It was a seminal moment in that year's Tour, and indeed in the rivalry between Armstrong and Ullrich – the moment when the American showed who was boss. Ullrich, totally demoralised by Armstrong's bluff, finished fully two minutes behind at the top of the Alpe.

When Armstrong convincingly won the following day's time trial, and followed it two days later with victory at St-Lary-Soulan, everybody knew that the Tour was won. A symbolic moment would follow as Ullrich gave one last effort in the stage to the mountain-top finish of

Luz-Ardiden, pursued all the way by Armstrong. As the two men reached the line together, they reached across and shook hands.

'I always say that you can never change someone's soul. There are virtues that I have kept: tenacity, aggression, love of hard work. But since my illness, my priorities have changed because I have been given a second chance. That is why I work so hard, why I am so determined. My illness taught me to make the most of the moment and to do everything within my power to make it as sweet as possible.'

Lance Armstrong

2001: ULLRICH TAKES A TUMBLE

Sometimes even the greatest bike riders can get it wrong. In 2001, during a hair-raising descent of the Col de Peyresourde, Jan Ullrich misread a hairpin bend and went somersaulting off the edge of the road and into a ravine. For a moment those with long memories thought back to the terrible day 41 years earlier when Roger Rivière broke his back in a similar incident. But Ullrich sprang to his feet with his bike over his shoulder, and, covered in mud and with his cycling kit in tatters, made it down the mountain to the finish.

TOUR TRIVIA

In 2001 four spectators were hurt at the stage finish in Colmar when a psychologically disturbed driver rammed his car through the barriers.

2002: SAME AGAIN FROM THE TEXAN

In 2002 it seemed all Lance Armstrong had to do was turn up to win his fourth consecutive Tour de France. Jan Ullrich, his only true rival the previous year, was missing with a knee injury and other than the Spanish climber Joseba Beloki, there appeared to be no other rider capable of challenging the American. The fears of the Tour organisers proved well-founded: Armstrong coasted to his easiest win yet. He set out his stall on the first day by winning the Prologue, then set his formidable US Postal team to work to ensure an armchair ride in the mountains. By the time he reached Paris, he had won four stages – including his now customary win in the final time trial – and was more than seven minutes ahead of Beloki. The prospect of him equalling the five victories of Anquetil, Merckx, Hinault and Indurain now seemed a formality. The only question at the end of three dominant weeks was just how many Tours Lance Armstrong could win.

'Armstrong to take six victories? The question may seem premature, but it's natural to ask it when you consider that when we look for a potential rival the cupboard seems decidedly bare.'

L'Équipe

TOUR PROFILE

Each stage has its own printed profile, which gives riders and spectators some indication of the route and its climbs. Above is a mountain stage profile from the 2006 stage from St-Jean-de-Maurienne to Morzine. It clearly shows the climbs, with height and gradient – and while the condensed nature of the distances makes it appear more steep than in reality, the profile still gives a good idea of the relentless nature of Tour de France mountain stages.

2002: THE MAN FROM OUAGADOUGOU

Michel Bationo is not a name instantly associated with the Tour de France, but in 2002 the man from Ouagadougou in Burkina Faso was given the great honour of being 'blackboard man'. In the days before earpieces and GPS satellite trackers, the blackboard man was a crucial part of the race, chalking time differences between breakaways and chasers on a blackboard while riding pillion on a motorcycle. While the job is more or less redundant now, some riders and team managers still like to see the blackboard, which is why it remains a part of the Tour.

Bationo, who had done the job in Burkina Faso's national tour for ten years, told a radio interviewer that it had always been his dream to work for the Tour de France. An official heard him and handed him the cherished blackboard for the 2002 Tour.

TOUR TRIVIA

In March 2003, less than four months before the start of the Tour, the Kazakh rider Andrei Kivilev died of head injuries sustained in a fall during his national championship. Following so soon after the death in similar circumstances of Fabio Casartelli (see Death of a Bike Rider, page 197), the Tour organisers made the decision to make safety helmets compulsory. They could only be removed at the foot-of-mountain finishes.

2003: A HUNDRED UP

The 2003 Tour marked the centenary of the event started by Henri Desgrange, and to celebrate the fact, the route recreated – as far as possible – the 1903 route. Indeed, a special prize – the *Centenaire Classement* – was created for the overall best-placed rider in the six stage finishes that matched those of the original Tour: Lyon, Marseille, Toulouse, Bordeaux, Nantes and Paris. It was won by Australia's Stuart O'Grady, with Thor Hushovd of Norway in second place.

Green	**Yellow**	**Polka dot**	**White**
Points winner	Winner	King of the Mountains	Best young rider

PODIUM

The final presentation in Paris is a chance for the winners of all four Tour jerseys to get together on the podium in front of the Arc de Triomphe.

TOUR TRIVIA

Apart from their bikes, the most important item in a rider's armoury is his Tour de France Roadbook, which contains details of every town, climb, sprint and key point of every stage on the route.

2003: CRASH!

The bunch sprint into Mcaux at the end of the first stage of the 2003 Tour saw Alessandro Petacchi stake his claim as the successor to fellow

Italian sprint king Mario Cipollini. But all eyes were fixed further down the finishing straight, where a touch of wheels at more than 40 mph (60 kph) had resulted in a spectacular and frightening crash involving more than 20 riders. Among them was Lance Armstrong, who was lucky to emerge with just a bruised leg and a grazed arm. Less fortunate was Armstrong's former team-mate Tyler Hamilton, now riding for the CSC team, who broke his collarbone.

TOUR TRIVIA

Alessandro Petacchi was the undoubted sprint king of 2003. Not only did he win four stages of the Tour de France, but he earlier bagged six stages of the Giro d'Italia. Like his predecessor Mario Cipollini, Petacchi was unabashed as he climbed off his bike at the first mountain stage, his work done for the year.

2003: THE TALE OF TYLER'S TEETH

Tyler Hamilton was no stranger to suffering. In the previous year's Giro, he had broken his left shoulder in a crash, but rather than quit, he carried on for several more stages. Such was the pain, Hamilton later needed dental treatment to fix the splintered enamel caused by grinding his teeth together. Tyler's teeth were in danger once again in 2003 when he rode the entire Tour after breaking his collarbone on stage one. With the broken bones held together with strapping, and unable to get out of his saddle because of the pain, Hamilton delivered a remarkable performance not only to survive but to mount a serious challenge to Armstrong in the mountains and win a superb solo stage into Bayonne. His achievement in coming fourth in the General

Classification was a display of bloody-minded determination of which the late Henri Desgrange would have been proud. Pity, then, that within a few months his reputation as one of the sport's good guys would be ripped to shreds.

2003: CROSS-COUNTRY

Lance Armstrong was no mean mountain-biker in his youth – and he showed he'd lost none of his old prowess with an astonishing feat of bike-handling during the long descent into Gap on stage nine. The tarmac on the winding mountain road had almost liquefied in the burning July heat, so much so that it not only caused Joseba Beloki to skid as he braked into a corner, but scorched the tyres from the rims of his wheels.

The Spaniard hit the road with a sickening thump; less than a bike length behind him, Armstrong had to wrench his handlebars to the left in order to avoid a collision. The next thing he knew, the American had left the road and was bumping across a field. Keeping his cool, Armstrong somehow managed to remain upright and guide his machine for 100 m down a steep, rutted wasteground. At the bottom of the field was a ditch separating it from the road. Armstrong calmly dismounted, swung his bike onto the road, jumped after it and climbed back into the saddle. If he lost any time at all, it was negligible. Indeed, the rest of the peloton were so amazed at the Texan's bike-handling skills that they were too awestruck to counter-attack. Back up the road, Beloki was not so fortunate: he had broken his femur, elbow and wrist and would spend more than a year recovering from his injuries.

2003: THE MUSETTE OF DOOM

If Armstrong thought his worries were over after surviving the huge pile-up on stage one, a succession of attacks by his rivals on stage eight to Alpe d'Huez, and a cross-country jaunt on stage nine, then he was wrong. On stage fifteen in the Pyrenees, the American faced one of his toughest ever days in the saddle – and in overcoming it proved he was a champion worthy of being included alongside the Tour's greatest names.

The trouble began on the slopes of the Tourmalet, when Armstrong once again found himself under constant sniping attack from Alexandre Vinokourov and his old sparring partner Jan Ullrich. Having survived that, Armstrong found himself at the foot of the 5,643 ft (1,720 m) climb to the finish at Luz-Ardiden with another rival, Iban Mayo. As the two men climbed shoulder to shoulder, Armstrong's right handlebar somehow snagged on a *musette* bag belonging to a roadside spectator. In an instant, the American was down on the road, with Mayo tumbling after him. Jan Ullrich, following only a few yards behind, managed to avoid the chaos and continued up the road. It was a real chance for the German to escape, but obeying the unwritten rule of the road, both he and Tyler Hamilton waited for the yellow jersey to get back on his bike. Armstrong, pumped up with adrenaline, soon caught them up. But a few moments later disaster almost struck again, when his feet slipped from his pedals and he landed painfully on his crossbar. Somehow the American not only managed to stay upright, but rallied himself for a devastating attack that left the rest floundering in his wake. Bloodshot and exhausted, Armstrong crossed the line a full 40 seconds ahead of the next rider.

'I took a corner too tight, got too close to the public… It was my fault and I couldn't do a thing about it. I said to myself, "Shit! This can't be happening! Not now!" I tried to get up as quickly as I could, saw I wasn't hurt apart from a cut on my elbow, checked the bike over, put the chain back on and set off. At times like that, instinct takes over.'

Lance Armstrong describes his crash on Luz-Ardiden

'He's accelerating again, Phil! This is amazing! This man has been on the ground, he almost lost his manhood on the crossbar of his bike a few moments ago, and now he's decided he wants to go!'

Paul Sherwen, British commentator, describes Armstrong's remarkable break to win the stage at Luz-Ardiden

TOUR TRIVIA
Armstrong's win in 2003 gained him membership of the Tour's exclusive Five Club. Fittingly, the surviving five-times winners of the Tour – Eddy Merckx, Bernard Hinault and Miguel Indurain – were at the finish line in Paris to greet the American.

TOUR TRIVIA
The 2003 Tour was the first which Lance Armstrong did not win by more than six minutes.

2004: BUSINESS AS USUAL

At the end of a hugely stressful Tour in 2003, Lance Armstrong announced, 'I don't ever want to go through another Tour like this.' In truth, he never had to. In 2004 the expected challenge from Ullrich and Hamilton never materialised, Iban Mayo was injured in an early crash, and Joseba Beloki was still recovering from his horrendous crash of the previous year. Indeed, only two riders dared to raise their heads above the parapet: Italy's Ivan Basso and the young Frenchman Thomas Voeckler. Basso gave as good as he got in the mountains, snatching a stage from Armstrong at La Mongie. Voeckler, meanwhile, won the hearts of all Frenchmen by holding on to the yellow jersey for ten days to win the Best Young Rider award.

2004: HAMILTON CRACKS

After his heroics a year earlier when he managed to come fourth despite a broken collarbone, Tyler Hamilton was forced to quit with back pain after another crash on stage six. Few suspected it would be the last the Tour would see of the American. Two months later, traces of EPO were found in his blood samples and he was banned for two years, despite claiming – bizarrely – that the dodgy readings were due to the fact that a twin brother had died in his mother's womb. A more prosaic reason for the results was suggested in 2006, however, when Spanish police carrying out Operation Puerto (see Operation Puerto, page 247) found Hamilton's name in the treatment log of 'dope doctor' Eufemiano Fuentes. The saga continues, but with Hamilton now 35 years old, the chances of him riding the Tour again seem remote even if he were to clear his name.

2004: THE ALPE PROVES DECISIVE

In a bid to stop Armstrong, or at least make his progress towards a sixth Tour victory slightly less than regal, the organisers loaded the last week of the race with some tough Alpine stages. The hope was that by then, notoriously slow starters like Ullrich would have ridden themselves into form and would be able to give the American a fight. Unfortunately, by the third week Armstrong was invincible. He proved it on the much-anticipated time trial up the Alpe d'Huez. Despite being barracked every metre by crowds hostile not only to him but to America in general, Armstrong flew up the mountain, catching Ivan Basso who had started two minutes before him. Ullrich, despite coming second, lost 61 seconds and with it any chance of winning the Tour.

TOUR TRIVIA

Jan Ullrich's fourth place in 2004 was the first time the German had finished lower than second in the Tour since winning on his debut in 1997.

TOUR TRIVIA

Richard Virenque, once vilified for his dope-taking in the Festina Affair of 1998, won his seventh King of the Mountains title, a Tour record.

☆ TOUR STARS WHO DIED IN 2004

Marco Pantani, aged 33: Pantani was one of the most gifted climbers of all time, the man who set the record for the climb up the Alpe d'Huez.

His Tour win in 1998 would prove to be the pinnacle of his career, however. The following year he was kicked out of the Giro d'Italia for doping offences, and as he strove to clear his name, his career and his mental health nosedived. He was found dead in a squalid hotel room on Valentine's Day 2004, apparently of a massive cocaine overdose.

2005: OVER AND OUT

If ever a Tour was over before it started it was the 2005 edition. The Prologue, rather than a short burst as usual, was a 12 mile (19 km) lung-burster which left the French mainland for the Île de Noirmoutier. It was here, in 1999, that the slippery causeway caused a massive pile-up and wrecked the chances of many of the pre-race favourites (see Road To Hell, page 224). This year the organisers took the sensible precaution of sending the riders over the road bridge instead. With 2.5 miles (4 km) to go, Lance Armstrong caught and overtook the bemused Jan Ullrich, who had started a minute ahead of him. It was a devastating blow for Ullrich, who was yet again being touted as a rival to the American despite a crash earlier in the season. Armstrong finished two seconds down on fellow countryman Dave Zabriskie, but Ullrich finished over a minute down as did the other main contenders, Ivan Basso, Iban Mayo, and Andreas Kloden, who had finished runner-up to Armstrong in 2004.

TOUR TRIVIA

Dave Zabriskie's startling average Prologue speed of 33.975 mph (54.676 kph) was the second fastest in history behind that of Britain's Chris Boardman in 1994. It's worth considering, however, that

Boardman's 34.271 mph (55.152 kph) was set over just 4.4 miles (7.2 km) – fully 7.4 miles (12 km) less than Zabriskie's.

2005: ZABRISKIE HEARTBREAK

Having held onto the yellow jersey for three days, Dave Zabriskie of the CSC team was confident that he would still have it after the team time trial on stage four. And he surely would have done, had he not crashed agonisingly into the advertising hoardings with just a couple of kilometres to go. That gave US Postal the win and Armstrong the yellow jersey. It was now just a matter of time before win number seven was notched up.

2005: THE FINAL CURTAIN

Unlike previous years, Lance Armstrong did not win any mountain stages in 2005. He didn't have to. With so many of his main rivals already out of the reckoning, all Armstrong had to do was ensure he stayed in touch. It would not have been an Armstrong victory without a time-trial success, however, and it was fitting that the great man's final Tour de France stage win came on the penultimate day's 34 mile (55 km) individual race against the clock.

2005: RASMUSSEN'S NIGHTMARE

Michael Rasmussen of Denmark was a surprising, but deserving winner of the King of the Mountains jersey. On the flat, however, he was a disaster. In the final time trial, needing only to finish with a half-decent time to secure a podium position, Rasmussen crashed after four kilometres, was forced to change his bike twice, his wheels twice, and then compounded his misery by pedalling into a ditch. His ride from hell dropped him from third to seventh overall.

'Our country and the world are incredibly proud of you. Your victory is a great triumph of the human spirit and a testament not only to your athletic talent but your courage.'

President George W. Bush congratulates Lance Armstrong on his unprecedented seventh Tour victory

'And finally the last thing I'll say for people who don't believe in cycling, the cynics and the sceptics: I'm sorry for you, I'm sorry you can't dream big, and I'm sorry you don't believe in miracles. But this is one hell of a race, this is a great sporting event and you should stand around and believe. You should believe in these athletes and you should believe in these people. And I'm a fan of the Tour de France for as long as I live and there are no secrets. This is a hard sporting event and hard work wins it, so *vive le tour*, for ever. Thank you.'

Lance Armstrong's speech from the podium in Paris after his seventh and final Tour win in 2005

☆ TOUR STARS WHO DIED IN 2005

Charly Gaul, aged 72: One of the most gifted yet flawed of riders, Charly Gaul of Luxembourg rode ten Tours between 1953 and 1963, winning in 1958. Gaul was a climber who earned his soubriquet 'Angel of the Mountains' by his superlative performances in the mountains in the mid-1950s. His career, however, was hampered by his inability to perform in the heat – a factor generally attributed to his use of amphetamines. Indeed, on more than one occasion he was seen to foam at the mouth as he rode flat stages in the baking sunshine. After retirement in 1965, Gaul became a virtual recluse, living in a caravan without electricity or running water and with only a dog for company.

It was only in 1983, after marrying for a third time, that he resurfaced – and many people were shocked by how the whippet-thin climber with the vast female fan club had transformed into a shambolic, pot-bellied figure with a huge beard. To its credit, the Tour organisers did their best to re-integrate one of its most famous sons into the real world. Towards the end of his life, Gaul became a regular figure alongside legends like Merckx and Hinault greeting the winners on the podium – and even if at times he didn't appear to know exactly where he was, at least he looked happy for the first time in decades.

2006: OPERATION PUERTO

With Lance Armstrong gone, the 2006 Tour promised to be the most competitive for years. Pre-race favourites were the young Italian rider Ivan Basso, fresh from his Giro win, Francesco Mancebo of Spain, the livewire Kazakh Alexandre Vinokourov, and of course Jan Ullrich. Yet on the eve of the race, all four were on their way home after a bombshell that threatened to derail the Tour and mire the world's greatest cycling event in its biggest scandal since the 1998 Festina Affair.

Operation Puerto was an investigation launched by Spanish police into doping in sport. The probe focussed in particular on the activities of Eufemiano Fuentes, a doctor specialising in the treatment of sportsmen. Raids on his flat unearthed more than 100 packets of blood, plus the equipment necessary to transfuse it. Police also found lists detailing Fuentes' clients and the dates when they had been treated. Although the individuals had been given nicknames to hide their true identities, it didn't take a genius to work out that 'Son of Rudy' was Jan Ullrich (managed by Rudy Pevenage) and that 'Birillo' was the name of Ivan Basso's dog.

In all, more than 200 athletes were implicated in the investigation. Of those, 56 were cyclists including such stars as Joseba Beloki, Francesco Mancebo, David Extabarria and Oscar Sevilla.

With the storm about to break, the team managers and Tour organisers acted fast. The day before the Prologue, Ullrich, Basso and Mancebo were withdrawn from the race. When Vinokourov was forced to withdraw on a technicality after most of his Astana-Wurth team were also named in the investigation, it meant that all of the top-five riders in the 2005 Tour would be missing in 2006.

It was a baptism of fire for the new Tour director Christian Prudhomme, who announced optimistically that 'shorn of favourites, instead [the race] is more open than ever'.

As the smallest field for more than 20 years set off from Strasbourg, little did Prudhomme know that his problems were only just beginning.

2006: THE CARDBOARD HAND OF FATE

When Norway's Thor Hushovd blasted to victory in the Prologue, the Tour organisers rejoiced that at last they could put the unsavoury events of Operation Puerto behind them. Their relief was to prove temporary, however. The following day Hushovd's right arm was sliced open by the razor-sharp edge of a green cardboard hand being waved by a spectator near the finish. A few years earlier, these giant hands had been banned after a similar incident involving Robbie McEwen, but in 2006 they had been reinstated – by the Tour organisers. With pictures of bloodsoaked Hushovd being beamed around the world, the hands were swiftly banned once again.

TOUR TRIVIA

The yellow jersey was worn by no less than seven different riders during the three-week, 20-stage race. They were: Thor Hushovd (Prologue and stage one), George Hincapie (stage two), Thor Hushovd (stage three), Tom Boonen (stages four–seven), Sergiy Honchar (stages eight–ten), Cyril Dessel (stage eleven), Floyd Landis (stages twelve–thirteen), Oscar Pereiro (stages fourteen–fifteen) Floyd Landis (stage sixteen), Oscar Pereiro (stages seventeen–eighteen), Floyd Landis (stages nineteen–twenty).

TOUR TRIVIA

Following his withdrawal from the Tour, Jan Ullrich was subsequently sacked by his T-Mobile team. From being firm favourite to win his second Tour, the German suddenly found that his career was all but over.

2006: LANDIS' HIP HORROR

As the race approached the mountains, American Floyd Landis – now one of the favourites – stunned everyone when he announced that immediately after the Tour he would be checking into hospital for a hip replacement. He revealed that following a crash in 2002, his right hip joint had degenerated to the extent that the bone was effectively dead, and that he had been riding in severe pain for almost a year.

TOUR TRIVIA
Due to an earlier operation on his dodgy hip, Floyd Landis's right leg is one inch shorter than his left.

2006: THE PELOTON PLAYS DUMB

One consequence of the mass expulsions prior to the Tour was that the peloton, shorn of its leaders, spent most of its time in a state of utter confusion. Never was this better illustrated than on stage thirteen, a rolling 142 miles (230 km) between Béziers and Montélimar, when a group of five riders escaped after 12 miles (20 km). The peloton, including race leader Floyd Landis, first ignored the break, then dithered about whether to chase and who should do the chasing. In the meantime, the breakaway group had extended their lead to a whopping 30 minutes. It was only when he arrived at the finish that Landis realised he had lost the yellow jersey by 90 seconds to Spanish rider Oscar Pereiro. As miscalculations go, this was one of the biggest in Tour history. The true significance of Pereiro's climb up the General Classification would only become clear after the race was over.

TOUR TRIVIA
Floyd Landis was raised in a strict Mennonite community in Pennsylvania. His parents regarded bike riding as a waste of time, and the wearing of Lycra as a sin. The young Floyd was forced to train by

sneaking out of his bedroom window at 1am in order to get the miles in before breakfast.

2006: PURGATORY

After regaining the yellow jersey two days after losing it to the upstart Oscar Pereiro, Floyd Landis was now firm favourite to retain it all the way to Paris. But this was to be a Tour of shocks – and on stage sixteen fate did not fail to deliver. A brutal Alpine stage, which included the ascents of the Galibier and the Croix-de-Fer, the final climb of the day was the relatively tame summit finish of La Toussuire. It was on this climb that Landis unexpectedly and spectacularly cracked. As the American ground his way towards the line at a snail's pace, eventually finishing 23rd, Pereiro took advantage to steam away and steal the yellow jersey once again. From leading the race, Landis was now back in eleventh position, nearly ten minutes behind and with his hopes of a Tour win seemingly in tatters.

2006: REDEMPTION

After consoling himself with what he said were just a couple of beers the night before, Floyd Landis set about regaining his yellow jersey for the second time on the mountainous stage from St-Jean-de-Maurienne to Morzine. What followed was one of the greatest solo breakaways of all time as the American blasted over the Col de Joux-Plane and then into Morzine to finish more than seven minutes ahead of Pereiro after an escape of 74 miles (120 km). Although the Spaniard still held on to yellow, his lead was now just twelve seconds with a time trial to follow.

Sure enough, Landis burned Pereira by over a minute to take an unassailable grip on the Tour as it headed for Paris. But as the Tour and the world were about to discover, the cloud of scandal that had hung over it from day one was about to erupt once again.

2006: WHAT A DOPE

Reeling from the hammer blow of Operation Puerto, the Tour had somehow rallied to produce one of the most exciting races in modern history. Or so it seemed. Just days after Floyd Landis rolled victorious into Paris, the event was dealt another haymaker by the news that the American had tested positive for illegal amounts of testosterone in his bloodstream. Not only that, but the test had been conducted immediately after Landis' epic 74 mile (120 km) breakaway to Morzine which set up his eventual victory. As an explanation for how he had managed to transform himself from the broken figure of the previous day into an unstoppable cycling machine, it suddenly seemed far more plausible than 'a couple of beers'.

'On that day, like 99 per cent of race followers said it was fantastic. Today I'm upset, but I remain convinced that the riders are capable of this kind of exploit without cheating.'

Christian Prudhomme, Tour director, reflects on Floyd Landis's win in Morzine and his subsequent doping charge

TOUR WINNERS 1999–2006

1999: Lance Armstrong (USA), [KoM: Richard Virenque (FRA); Points: Erik Zabel (GER)]

2000: Lance Armstrong (USA), [KoM: Santiago Botero (COL); Points: Erik Zabel (GER)]

2001: Lance Armstrong (USA), [KoM: Laurent Jalabert (FRA); Points: Erik Zabel (GER)]

2002: Lance Armstrong (USA), [KoM: Laurent Jalabert (FRA); Points: Robbie McEwen (AUS)]

2003: Lance Armstrong (USA), [KoM: Richard Virenque (FRA); Points: Baden Cooke (AUS)]

2004: Lance Armstrong (USA), [KoM: Richard Virenque (FRA); Points: Robbie McEwen (AUS)]

2005: Lance Armstrong (USA), [KoM: Michael Rasmussen (DEN); Points: Thor Hushovd (NOR)]

2006: Floyd Landis (USA)*, [KoM: Michael Rasmussen (DEN); Points: Robbie McEwen (AUS)]

* Final result contested at the time of writing.

THE BRITISH ARE COMING...AND THE IRON MAN IS BACK

2007-2009

2007: CRASH LANDIS

To be kicked off the Tour for doping is bad enough – but to have actually been crowned winner on the Champs Elysees beforehand is a blow from which few riders could ever hope to recover. Perhaps this explains Floyd Landis's obsessional quest to clear his name, despite seemingly irrefutable evidence that his epic 74–mile solo breakaway in the Alps was fuelled by an illegal dose of testosterone. With both A and B tests coming back positive, and having been sacked by his team Phonak (which itself subsequently folded), perhaps the American felt he had nothing to lose. What transpired was a painful legal battle that dragged on for nearly eighteen months after the event. It also meant that on the eve of the 2007 Tour the matter was still unresolved, leaving the event without a reigning champion.

2007: BJARNE COMES CLEAN...EVENTUALLY

Bjarne Riis, winner of the 1996 Tour and latterly directeur sportif of the powerful CSC team, is a taciturn man at the best of times. Which makes his unprompted confession, on the eve of the Tour and eleven years after the event, that he was doped up to the eyeballs with EPO, growth hormone and cortisone during his triumph even more bizarre. Admittedly several of Riis's former Telekom team–mates had begun spilling the beans prior to the Eagle of Denmark's admission – but still, if he'd kept quiet he could have remained under the same cloud of unproven suspicion hanging over every Tour winner since 1903. Riis was immediately expunged from the record books – only to be reinstated a year later, his name asterisked and copious explanatory notes attached.

2007: YOU WAIT FOR ONE DOPE...

As the Tour approached, it seemed an orderly queue was required to sort out the sudden influx of bent riders being exposed by both Operacion Puerto and the markedly improved dope testing techniques employed by the ICU. And it seemed that, if they could nail the Tour winner himself, the authorities were not going to hold any truck with reputation. In quick succession out went Giro winner Danilo Di Luca, Tour favourite Ivan Basso, and top sprinter Alessandro Petacchi. The question on everyone's lips – would there be anyone left to ride the 2007 Tour?

'Having the Grand Départ on the seventh of July will broadcast to the
world that terrorism does not shake our city.'

Ken Livingstone, Mayor of London in 2007.

2007: LONDON LIFT–OFF

After all the hype, the 2007 Tour de France began with a scenic 7.9km
(5 mile) time trial course from Whitehall to The Mall, taking in
Parliament Square, Victoria Street, Buckingham Gate and Constitution
Hill en route. The first rider out of the blocks was number 214, Enrico
Degano from Italy. British hopes rested with Bradley Wiggins – but in
the event world time trial champion Fabian Cancellara blew everyone
away with a time of 8m 50s to grab the first maillot jaune of the Tour.
Wiggins himself finished a respectable fourth.

2007: MEET LANCE

Giant screens were erected in Hyde Park to beam live coverage of the
Prologue to hundreds of thousands of visitors. But the undoubted
highlight of the day for most people was chance to get their picture
taken with a Madame Tussaud's waxwork of Tour legend Lance
Armstrong.

2007: POLICE PRESENCE

Mayor Livingstone's message of defiance to the terrorists was all very well – but as the Tour left London bound for its first stage stop in Canterbury, the police were taking no chances. Over 4,500 British officers and forty–five of their French counterparts took up high profile positions close to the crowds of spectators along the 203 km (126 miles) route.

2007: DAVE STEALS CAV'S THUNDER

Stage 1 of the Tour was destined to be home–grown Mark Cavendish's day of glory – a flat stage culminating in a bunch sprint in Canterbury. But the Tour has a habit of making fools of anyone who tries to make predictions, and so it proved. While the young Manxman endured a day of mechanical frustrations and trailed in with the peloton and on a replacement bike, it was forgotten man Dave Millar who grabbed the headlines by leading a breakaway that ultimately earned him the King of the Mountains jersey for the day.

2007: THANKS FOR COMING, EDUARDO

Poor old Eduardo Gonzalez Ramires. All that training, all that expectation, and for what? The Spaniard became the Tour's first retirement just a couple of hours into the first stage when he collided with a support car, smashed its windscreen, and in the process damaged himself to the extent that he could no longer continue in the race.

2007: WIGGO'S BREAKAWAY TRIBUTE

The shadow of the late Tom Simpson continues to hang over British road racing, and Stage 6 of this year's Tour coincided with the 40th anniversary of the County Durham–born cyclist's death on Mont Ventoux. Was it any coincidence, therefore, that Bradley Wiggins should choose this stage to launch a stirring solo breakaway on the 200km (124 miles) flat stage to Bourg en Bresse? Wiggins, who shot clear after just two kilometres, denied it – but by staying away until just seven kilometres to go he had produced a performance of which Mr Tom himself would have been proud.

2007: CAV CLIMBS OFF

There had been great hopes for Mark Cavendish – but this was not to be his year. After just two top–10 finishes in the sprints and two nasty crashes in the first week, he gamely struggled through two days in Alps before climbing off his bike on Stage 8.

2007: WHO LET THE DOGS OUT?

One of the great joys of the Tour is its all–inclusiveness. It costs nothing to watch, there are no roadside restrictions, and you can even bring your dog. Just keep it on its lead, though – because as far as cyclists are concerned, there is no such thing as a four–legged friend. Ask Marcus Burghardt. On Stage 9 of the race, the German rider's day in the saddle was rudely interrupted when a particularly dopey–looking golden retriever sauntered into the road. Burghardt hit the dog, his front wheel buckled, and he was flung over his handlebars. While heading a breakaway on Stage 18, meanwhile, both Sandy Casar and Frederik Willems were sent flying when a mutt shot across their path. Fortunately both riders and dogs lived to fight another day – Casar even got back on his bike and won the stage.

2007: THE UNRAVELLING OF RASMUSSEN

Michael Rasmussen not only won King of the Mountains in 2005 and 2006, he captured everyone's heart with his comedy of errors in the time trialling. In 2007, however, there was to be only contempt for the skeletal Dane as he brought the legendary maillot jaune into disrepute for the second year running.

Trouble began just hours after Rasmussen had secured yellow with a blistering ascent into Tignes on Stage 8. News filtered through that he had been dropped by his national team for failing to report for mandatory drugs tests earlier that year, an allegation the rider blamed on an 'administrative mistake'. Despite the initial support of organiser Christian Prudhomme, the rug was pulled from under Rasmussen's feet shortly afterwards – by his own team, Rabobank, who unceremoniously sacked him and withdrew from the race. It seemed they were not convinced by his excuses and were unwilling to take the risk of being associated with a high–profile doper. The look of stunned astonishment on Rasmussen's face summed up how Tour cheats suddenly had nowhere to hide – and he was not to be the last big name to fall foul of the zero tolerance approach.

'I think it's a great day. If we didn't have this out–of–competition testing this would never have arisen. He was playing the system. The system is not foolproof but it's getting better, and that's proven.'

David Millar, himself a former doper, welcomes the demise of Michael Rasmussen.

2007: IF IT SEEMS TOO GOOD TO BE TRUE, IT PROBABLY IS

Alexandre Vinokourov had been one of the pre–race favourites, but a nasty crash had left the powerful Azerbaijani struggling to keep up in the general classification. That all changed with a stunning victory in the second individual time trial, followed two days later by an equally impressive stage win in the Pyrenees. But if it seemed like a remarkable turnaround, there was an equally predictable explanation. Blood tests revealed Vinokourov had received an illegal blood transfusion prior to the time trial. The rider blamed the physical effects of his crash – but nobody was buying it, least of all his team Astana. Like Rabobank, they immediately withdrew from the race, leaving Vino high and dry, and the Tour in a now familiar state of chaos.

'I think it's a mistake in part due to my crash. I have spoken to the team doctors who had a hypothesis that there was an enormous amount of blood in my thighs, which could have led to my positive test.' – Vinokourov's frankly baffling excuse for his positive dope test.

2007: MORENI – GUILTY AS CHARGED

After the pitiful excuses of Rasmussen and Vinokourov, it was almost a relief when Christophe Moreni admitted he was a cheat. Tested positive on Stage 11 and arrested by gendarmes after Stage 16, Moreni came clean immediately without waiting for a second test to confirm his guilt. His team Cofidis followed the lead of Astana and Rabobank and withdrew from the race, which was bad news for team mate Bradley Wiggins, who after an excellent Tour found himself prematurely on the plane home.

'No–one has faith in who is wearing the yellow jersey. This year's Tour has lost all credibility. It's null and void as far as I am concerned this year.' – a distraught Bradley Wiggins after his Cofidis team withdrew from the Tour.

2007: DEATH NOTICES

The French Press were in no doubt that this latest batch of disqualifications signalled the end of the Tour as a viable sporting event:

'Death notice: the Tour de France died on 25 July 2007, at the age of 104, after a long illness…The Tour is clinically dead. It is a broken toy, a burst soap bubble popped by careless kids, unaware that they are damaging themselves, their health and their childhood dreams as well. It's all the more painful as we had almost begun to believe in the Tour again… in these soap–and–water cyclists who we were so ready to love. But instead of dreams, the last 48 hours have been a living nightmare.'

France Soir

'It really doesn't matter who wins the Tour. The 2007 edition died on 24 July on the heights of Loudenvielle. Killed by Alexandre Vinokourov, idolised by the media and cycling fans, but revealed to have the blood of another running in his veins on the finishing line. Damn Vinokourov! He sullied the infinite beauty of the Pyrenees, dirtied cycling a little more and further discredited the Tour de France.'

Le Figaro

2007: OH…AND ER, CONTADOR WON

Alberto Contador, at 24, became the youngest winner of the Tour since Jan Ullrich and the first Spanish victor since Miguel Indurain in 1995 as the race finally limped into Paris after arguably the most traumatic three weeks in its history. The overall mood of despondency was a far cry from the celebratory scenes in London, and even the event's most ardent fans were struggling to see any point in carrying on. But with a raft of big names either banned or deciding to retire before the drug controls caught up with them, the field was now open for a new generation of riders not brought up in the culture of cheating – and, miraculously, the beacon of hope would be passed to a former bank clerk from Douglas, in the Isle of Man…

TOUR TRIVIA

Alberto Contador's margin of victory (23 seconds) was the narrowest since Greg Lemond beat Laurent Fignon by eight seconds in 1989.

2008: A STAR IS BORN

At the start of his Tour de France career things did not look promising for Mark Cavendish. For a start he was a British–born sprinter, and there hadn't been a successful one of those since Barry Hoban back in the 1960s. Secondly, he had looked hopelessly out of his depth in the pro peloton, failing to finish almost every race he took part in for T–Mobile at the start of his maiden 2007 season.

But Cavendish, already a gold medal–winning track star, had one thing going for him – and that was an almost supernatural belief in his own ability. Sure enough, as the 2007 season continued, the lad from the Isle of Man began to come good. Wins at the Four Days of Dunkirk and the Volta a Catalunya propelled him into the T–Mobile Tour team, and while he never finished higher than ninth during the race, and climbed off after two days in the Alps, it was experience that was to prove hugely valuable.

In 2008, riding now for the powerful Team Columbia, Cav proved he was no flash in the pan, winning two stages of the Giro d'Italia early in the season. But this was an Olympic year, and with the prospect of track medals looming it was a question of just how much preparation he would be able to devote to the Tour. To the delight of everyone associated with the sport in the UK, the 23–year–old would provide the answer in emphatic fashion.

'To be honest, he started the season so catastrophically that the staff were wondering what they could enter Mark for so that he could finish the race.' – Team mate Roger Hammond describing Mark Cavendish's unspectacular start to 2007.

2008: ALL CHANGE FOR THE TOUR

It may have seemed like an attempt to paper over the gaping cracks, but even as the controversy surrounding the previous year's Tour raged on, the event organisers unveiled the route of the 2008 edition, promising sweeping Henri Desgrange–style changes in a bid to make the tarnished event more exciting.

Time bonuses were scrapped and, for the first time since 1966, the race would not start with a solo time trial, but with a 195km opening stage. The route would also include Europe's highest mountain pass; the 2,802–metre Col de la Bonette–Restefond. What really had aficionados licking their lips, however, was the brutal climb up Alpe d'Huez on the penultimate day, designed to keep the race alive to the very last and prevent the winner being decided a week before the finish.

Vive le Tour!

'We want the Tour to rediscover its romanticism,' said Tour director Christian Prudhomme. But there would be steel behind the gloss. Also introduced for 2008 was a raft of hard–hitting anti–doping measures. No rider would be allowed to start without first agreeing to take part in a series of tests aimed at building a blood profile for each athlete. If follow–up tests showed significant changes to that profile – which could be caused by drug use – riders faced being barred from racing for up to four years.

One rider who saved the testers the trouble was Tom Boonen. The talented Belgian was banned weeks before the Grande Depart after testing positive for cocaine.

2008: CRASH, BANG, WALLOP

After all the travails about drug testing it was almost reassuring to see that some things about the Tour remained the same – namely, ridiculous crashes on Stage 1. Usually these are down to nerves, but there was little Tour debutant Herve Duclos–Lasalle could do about the musette bag that got caught in his spokes at a midway feed station, ejecting him from the saddle and putting him out of the race with a broken wrist.

TOUR TRIVIA

In 2002 Alberto Contador spent 10 days in a coma after suffering swelling to the brain following a crash in the Tour of Asturias.

2008: CAVENDISH STIRS

It had been 33 long years since Barry Hoban had powered to victory at the Bordeaux velodrome, thereby securing Britain's last bunch sprint win at the Tour – and to be honest, nobody had even come close to breaking the drought. But in Mark Cavendish there was at last a home–grown sprinter with the potential to make a name for himself among the world's best. His early season form had been sensational – but on the mammoth 233km (145 miles) fifth stage from Cholet to Chateauroux the Manx Bullet truly came of age. As the peloton hammered into town at speeds of up to 60kmh, Cavendish tucked himself into the back of his Team Columbia train and waited. As his pace–setters peeled away one–by–one, he found himself in the slipstream of Gerald Ciolek, a vastly experienced domestique. With 250m to go, Ciolek moved aside and Cavendish hit the front, legs pumping, chin grazing his handlebars. It was no contest. Despite the presence of such sprint kings as Thor Hushovd and Eric Zabel, the young Brit was unstoppable. As he punched the air in triumph, seasoned Tour observers knew that a star had been born.

TOUR TRIVIA

Prior to Mark Cavendish's win on Stage 5 of the 2008 Tour, the last British stage winner was David Millar, who grabbed first place in the 2003 time–trial in Nantes.

2008: THE COBRA LEGS IT

There was no greater admirer of Italian rider Riccardo Ricco than Ricco himself. After all here was a man who, aged just 24, called himself The Cobra and compared himself with the great climber Marco Pantani. After two impressive wins on stages six and nine in the mountains, however, it seemed he might have a point. But, as Floyd Landis, Michael Rasmussen and Alexandre Vinokourov had proved, great feats of endurance are not necessarily what they seem. And, when a routine dope test revealed Ricco to be swimming in EPO, it was with a certain amount of schadenfreude that the Cobra was found to be as big a cheat as his idol, Il Pirata. Ricco, of course, protested his innocence – but his case was somewhat undermined by his attempt to run away from the dope testers. His break for freedom was foiled by a traffic jam, and his Tour was over very shortly afterwards.

2008: RULED OUT BY THE RULES

As the peloton revs up for a bunch sprint, crashes are inevitable. According to the rulebook, however, any rider who comes down inside the last 3km is credited with the same time as the group he was in when he crashed – the idea being that the overall contenders should not have to battle to the front to get ahead of potential pile–ups in flat stage finishes. The same is not true in the mountains, though, as yellow jersey holder Stefan Schumacher discovered when he clipped Kim Kirchen's back wheel and fell just 300m short of the summit of Super–Besse. Riccardo Ricco sprinted away for the win and the maillot jaune, as Schumacher trailed in 32 seconds later.

2008: RECORDS FALL FOR CAV

Mark Cavendish won the eighth stage of the Tour de France to become only the second British rider to win two stages in the same Tour, following his dramatic victory in stage five. But he was far from finished. Victories on Stages 12 and 13, pouncing to perfection after the lead out from his Team Columbia train, made him the only British to take four stages – but Barry Hoban's record would stand for another year at least as the young sprinter, having struggled in the Pyrenees, climbed off his bike shortly after entering the Alps.

2008: CAR CATASTROPHE

Watching the Tour can sometimes be as risky as riding it. At the end of Stage 11 into Foix, two adults and two children were injured when the AG2R team car lost control and ran into the crowd huddled behind the barriers. All four casualties were taken to hospital, but thankfully their injuries were not serious.

2008: THE CODE OF HONOUR

The peloton is a mysterious and secretive beast that looks after its own, and this has often been blamed for the continuing drug abuse that has scarred the sport. But it's not all bad, as Denis Menchov discovered during an attempted solo breakaway in the mountains. As he powered around a corner, Menchov's front tyre skidded on some fresh paint applied to the road by fans, and down he went. Instead of leaving him for dead, however, the pursuing group slowed to allow the grateful Russian to remount and catch up.

TOUR TRIVIA

Barry Hoban was Britain's undisputed sprint king, with eight stage wins during his career. But while it took the Yorkshireman 11 years to clock up his tally, Mark Cavendish would supersede that total in just two.

2008: JOHN–LEE'S UP AND DOWN DAY

Towering at over 2,800m the Col de la Bonette–Restefond is the highest mountain pass in Europe, and before this year's Tour it had only been climbed on three occasions. So it was truly an honour for unknown 21–year–old South African John–Lee Augustyn to follow in the hallowed tyre tracks of the 'Eagle of Toledo' Federico Bahamontes (twice) and Scotland's own King of the Mountains Robert Millar and reach the summit first. Unfortunately John–Lee's moment of glory was to be followed less than a minute later by ignominy. Overcome by the occasion, perhaps – or most likely knackered after the climb – Augustyn undercooked a sweeping bend on the descent and went flying off the mountain. While he was fortunate the drop was a relatively shallow shale slope rather than a sheer cliff face, he still had to face the embarrassment of climbing back up it, covered in dust, only to discover that his bike had plunged out of sight down the mountain. Having crossed the summit in the lead, Augustyn had to wait for a replacement and would finish the stage in 35th position.

2008: THE ALPE DECIDES IT

The organisers of the Tour had hoped that the final mountain stage up the fearsomely steep hairpins of Alpe d'Huez would be decisive – and so it proved. With the likes of Cadel Evans and young Frank Schleck vying for the maillot jaune, it was the Spanish climber Carlos Sastre who timed his burst to perfection, sprinting away from the leaders 13km from the summit. He finished two minutes ahead of them, and with only a time trial to come before Paris his victory was assured.

TOUR TRIVIA

At the start of each stage, Parisian artist André Puzin begins work on a 5ft by 8ft watercolour depicting the current leaders. He gives himself an hour to complete his work, and the result is presented to the mayor of the ville départ.

2009: LIVESTRONG AND PROSPER?

Depending on who you believe, Lance Armstrong's shock decision to return to professional cycling – and to the Tour he had dominated for almost a decade – was prompted by a) his desire to publicise his cancer charity or b) the conviction that he still had what it took to beat the current crop of riders. Most likely it was c) a mixture of both. Whatever the reason, the great man's comeback was regarded with horror by some, who regarded him as a throwback to a murky era of drug scandals, but with huge excitement by most observers. Could he win an eighth Tour at the age of 37? Could he really become the oldest winner since Firmin Lambot in 1922?

'As with anything there is going to be up and downsides to it. There's going to be natural negative factors that you have to consider, but you sit down and you look at it and you think, on balance, this is a positive thing overall. That's the beauty of this comeback. You lay out different scenarios in your head. What if you won the Tour again? Or the Giro? Or if you won them both? Or you lost them both? You lay it all out and I'm still up for it.'

Seven–times Tour winner Lance Armstrong announces he will compete in the 2009 race after a four–year hiatus.

2009: BAD OMENS?

Lance Armstrong's return to the world of pro cycling was not quite as smooth as he had hoped. During the early season Tour of California someone pinched his time trial bike, and at the subsequent Vuelta a Castilla y Leon he crashed on Stage 1 and broke his collarbone. Typically, Armstrong was back on his bike just four days after an operation to repair the damage.

2009: GOOD OMENS?

While everyone's attention was focussed on Lance Armstrong's build–up to the 2009 Tour, one of the most remarkable cycling achievements of the year was almost overshadowed. The Milan–San Remo one day race is a traditional curtain raiser and one of the so–called Monuments of the sport. Previous winners include greats such as Eddie

Merckx, Fausto Coppi and Laurent Fignon. The only British victor was Tom Simpson in 1964 – until, against all expectations, Mark Cavendish came from nowhere to win the race with a quite brilliant ride. The man who just two years earlier couldn't even finish a race was now red hot favourite for the Tour's green points jersey.

2009: A PROLOGUE FIT FOR A PRINCE

After a year's absence the individual time trial prologue was back for the 2009 Tour, and the setting was the spectacular millionaire's playground of Monaco. With Prince Albert looking on, the lumpy 15.4 km (9.6 miles) course was gobbled up by the Swiss rider Fabian Cancellara, who repeated his performance two years earlier to take yellow. All eyes were on Armstrong, of course – and the American finished a creditable ninth.

'The controls will be multiplied and I tell Lance Armstrong that he will be particularly, particularly, particularly monitored.'

French sports minister **Roselyne Bachelot.**

2009: CAVENDISH ON FIRE

He'd promised last year and now he delivered in spades. Mark Cavendish was simply unstoppable in the early bunch sprints, winning stages 2 and 3 with ease and leaving his rivals for the points jersey, specifically big Thor Hushovd, gasping in his wake. But if Cav thought it was going to be a procession into Paris – and his ill–advised all–green bike, jersey and glasses combo suggested he did – then he was in for a rude awakening. The battle for green was only just beginning. And it was going to be an epic.

2009: THE CURSE OF CAV

The Manx Bullet was not entirely happy after his first stage win in Brignoles, claiming that he'd been punched in the kidneys en route by Dutch rider Kenny van Hummel. In fact it wasn't Van Hummel but his team–mate, Piet Rooijakkers. Two days later, Rooijakkers crashed, breaking his offending arm in three places, requiring seven hours of surgery, including a bone graft from his hip. Spooky...

TOUR TRIVIA

By tenaciously holding on to the yellow jersey until the Pyrenees on Stage 7, Fabian Cancellara achieved the distinction of wearing it for a career total of 13 days – longer than Swiss compatriots and former Tour winners Ferdy Kubler and Huger Koblet.

2009: THE OTHER BATTLE

As the Tour switched to the mountains, another intriguing subplot of the race came to the fore – namely, the battle for supremacy between Astana team–mates Lance Armstrong and Alberto Contador, both for the yellow jersey and the leadership of the team itself. The mutual distrust they shared for each other was no secret, but came to the fore when, on the climb to Arcalis, Contador took matters into his own hands and blitzed the final kilometre, leaving Armstrong floundering in his wake and in the general classification. The seven–times champ's face was a picture as he fumed beside the team bus. But the younger man had set down a challenge that would be hard to beat.

'The honest truth? There's a little tension at the table. For me, Alberto is very strong, very ambitious, and I understand that. I've won this race a lot so I don't care if I come second or third or fifth. It's OK. It's honestly OK. I try to relax and keep the atmosphere as cool as I can.'

Lance Armstrong shows he is the master of understatement after Contador's break to Arcalis.

2009: ANOTHER CAV DOUBLE

By storming to victory in Stages 10 and 11, Mark Cavendish equalled Barry Hoban's British record of eight career wins. He also wrested back the green jersey from Thor Hushovd, the powerful Norwegian, who had used all his Tour nous to accumulate intermediate points on the road to top the points table. The question now remained, could the young Manx sprinter hold onto the coveted jersey through the mountains? Or was there more drama ahead?

2009: A DEAF EAR FROM THE PELOTON

The old school of cycling – mainly Bernard Hinault – still maintains that radios connecting riders with their support cars goes against racing principles and makes the sport predictable. Not so the modern peloton, who have become so accustomed to the soothing voice of their directeur sportif in their ear that the idea of being without it is akin to blindfolding them. So when the Tour organisers announced earpieces were being banned on Stage 10 there was bound to be trouble, and so it proved. Of the 20 teams in the race, 14 protested, filing a petition to the sport's governing body and riding the stage at a leisurely pace. The result? A craven backdown by the organisers, who announced that plans to repeat the experiment on Stage 13 had been abandoned.

'Next they'll be asking us to ride for two days without helmets, or without cables in our brakes.'

Veteran German rider **Jens Voigt**, after the decision to ride two stages of the Tour without earpiece radios.

2009: A SHOT ACROSS THE BOWS

With their radios returned, the riders might have expected a smooth and safe ride as the peloton made its way over the Alps from St Gaudens to Tarbes. Not a bit of it. Garmin–Slipstream rider Julian Dean was hit on the hand by a pellet fired from an airgun. The same sniper also bagged Oscar Freire in the leg. Neither shooting proved serious, but in an event never short of incident this rates as a first.

TOUR TRIVIA

The talented Nicholas Roche, son of Irish Tour winner Stephen Roche, also thought he might have been shot after he was struck by a missile on the back of the leg. It turned out to be shrapnel from an exploding roadside ice compressor.

2009: ROADSIDE TRAGEDY

The previous year four people suffered minor injuries when a team car ploughed into the crowd. This year there were more serious consequences when a motorcycle ridden by a Tour official struck and killed a spectator as she crossed the road during the 14th Stage from Colmar to Besancon. The rider then fell off his bike, which hit and injured two other people, including a mother with a child in her arms. Fortunately they were not seriously hurt.

2009: CRUSHED BY THE GOD OF THUNDER

The battle for the green jersey, so often a sideshow compared to the battle for yellow, erupted spectacularly into controversy and recrimination on Stage 14. Mark Cavendish won the bunch sprint from Thor Hushovd, and therefore believed he had gained control of the jersey as the race headed into the Alps. But after complaints from Hushovd that the Manxman had tried to ride him into the barriers, Cavendish was stripped of his win – and the precious points he had earned on the stage. Video evidence suggested the decision was at the very least harsh, but there was no going back. Hushovd now led by 18 points, a near unassailable lead considering the few opportunities remaining for the incandescent Cavendish to claw it back.

'It was probably my worst ever day in cycling.'

Mark Cavendish reflects on the decision to
disqualify him from his Stage 14 win.

2009: WHAT ABOUT WIGGINS?

Mark Cavendish might have been grabbing all the headlines for his
sprinting exploits, but it was another British rider who had won the
hearts of the Tour spectators. Bradley Wiggins, who left the race a
disillusioned man after his Cofidis team's withdrawal in 2007, had
returned a slimmer and stronger road rider after ditching his track
career to concentrate on the Tour. And what a transformation it was!
Almost overnight it seemed Brad had transformed himself from a decent
time–triallist into a first–class all rounder. Most astonishing of all was
his ability to compete with the very best in the mountains and remain in
contention for the yellow jersey. Indeed for a brief time on Stage 16, as
the leaders slogged up the Col du Petit Saint–Bernard, he actually led
the race. He would eventually finish in fourth place in Paris, an
achievement of which he can be justly proud.

2009: ARMSTRONG ROLLS BACK THE YEARS

For a 37–year–old man competing in his first Tour for four years, Lance
Armstrong had performed heroically – but it seemed he could not top
the sheer youthful exuberance of his team–mate Alberto Contador, 11
years his junior. However the old man of the race was determined to
show he was not simply there to make up the numbers, and on Stage 16

he produced a display of brilliance that could have been taken from his glory days. Seemingly struggling to keep up on the Col du Petit Saint–Bernard, Armstrong suddenly summoned a burst of energy that saw him fly up the mountain to catch the leaders. It wasn't enough to win the stage or even put him in contention for the maillot jaune – but as a two–fingered salute to his critics it couldn't be bettered.

2009: HORROR CRASH FOR JENS

German rider Jens Voigt is one of the most popular and articulate riders in the peloton. So it was with horror that viewers watched as this tireless domestique crashed on the high–speed descent of the Col du Petit St Bernard. When you crash at speeds of up to 100kmh (60mph) the outcome is never going to be insignificant, and for a while, as Voigt lay motionless on the road with blood spilling across the tarmac, there were sickening memories of Fabio Casartelli's fatal crash on the Col de Portet d'Aspet in 1995. Fortunately, it looked a whole lot worse than it was. Voigt was out of the race with a fractured cheekbone and concussion – but once again the often perilous existence of the 'convicts of the road' was laid bare.

2009: TRUE GRIT SECURES THE RECORD

Like most sprinters Mark Cavendish is not known for his climbing ability, preferring to loiter at the back of the peloton when the Tour reaches the mountains. So his historic stage win in Aubenas, in which he superseded Barry Hoban's record of eight stage wins, was something extra special. Although designated a flat stage, there was a vicious second category hill just before the end that most sprinters would have balked at. Cav, however, had other ideas – and in the team bus before the race instructed his men to 'Just get me up the climb'. They did just that, and in a dramatic sprint for the line the Manxman pipped his rival Thor Hushovd to secure the sweetest of victories.

2009: PODIUM POOCH

Tour stage winners can usually look forward to a bottle of champagne and peck on the cheek from two attractive looking girls when they take to the winner's podium. After his magisterial and race–winning climb to victory in Verbier on Stage 15, however, Alberto Contador was also given a St Bernard dog.

2009: THE END OF THE ROAD FOR KENNY

If you aren't going to win the Tour, the next best thing is to come dead last. The so–called Lanterne Rouge is a prized accolade among the also–rans and winning it often takes as much skill and guile as winning the maillot jaune itself. This year Kenny Van Hummel's daily battle to cross the line inside the time limit made him a celebrity in his native Holland. And, trailing the leader Alberto Contador by a whopping three hours, 30 minutes in the overall standings it looked like he'd finally succeeded as the peloton set off on the routine 169km (105 miles) penultimate stage. But cycling is a cruel mistress, and having been dropped after just 4km, Van Hummel found himself in a race to catch up. And so it was that on a descent of the second hill of the day, the unfortunate Dutchman went flying over his handlebars after misjudging a corner. His knee was badly cut and, tragically, his Tour was over. As Van Hummel recuperated in hospital he could only watch and wonder what might have been as Belarusian Yauheni Hutarovich trailed into Paris and into immortality.

2009: THE ICING ON THE CAKE

It had already been a Tour to remember for Mark Cavendish who, along with the reborn Bradley Wiggins, had snatched all the limelight from Lance Armstrong and in the process stamped the Union Jack across the event for the first time since Tom Simpson. He might not have won the green jersey, but it was surely a case now of when rather than if. In the meantime he had established himself as Britain's greatest ever sprinter, and one of the best in the history of the event. But there remained one piece of unfinished business – and on a historic day in Paris nobody was going to come between Cavendish and a win on the Champs Elysees. Led out to perfection by his faithful Columbia team Cav motored clear by almost the length of the Champs itself and raised his fists in triumph as he crossed the line for the sixth time in the Tour.

2009: IF LOOKS COULD KILL

An intriguing postscript to the Tour was played on the winner's podium itself as the three top–placed riders in the general classification stood to receive their awards. While young Andy Schleck looked simply thrilled to have finished second in only his second Tour, it was the body language of the other two riders that caused the most interest. The simmering discontent between Alberto Contador and Lance Armstrong had never been in doubt during the race, but now their body language and the way neither man so much as glanced at each other left no–one in doubt that this was one rivalry that was not yet over.